To — Wanda McCutcheon — with best wishes [signature] 1989

Wanda - I hope you enjoy my friend's newest book on Oklahoma frontier history.

Merry Christmas!

[signature], Dec 25, 89

Purple Sage

Patrick Sylvester McGeeney as president of the Lone Star and the Shamrock Photoplay motion picture producing companies of San Antonio, Texas (1914–1923).

Purple Sage

The Exploits,
Adventures,
and Writings
of Patrick Sylvester McGeeney

by

Glenn Shirley

Barbed Wire Press
Stillwater, Oklahoma

Cover and book design by L.A. Smith

Published by Barbed Wire Press, P.O. Box 2107, Stillwater, OK 74076
Manufactured in the United States of America
First Edition

ISBN 0-935269-04-5

CONTENTS

ILLUSTRATIONS

Preface

For a full half-century, Patrick Sylvester McGeeney was known as "Purple Sage"—adventurer extraordinary. Born in Tyrone County, Ireland, he came to America with his parents when little more than a babe in arms and spent his boyhood in "bloody" Newton, Kansas, an end-of-track cowtown on the Chisholm Trail. Stagestruck from the time he entered his teens, he trouped with a stock company through Kansas, Indiana, and Ohio, achieving a modicum of success, which led finally to the rosy paths of acting and motion picture production.

McGeeney first stepped into adventure at age nineteen when, as a brakeman for the Santa Fe railroad with runs through the old Cherokee Outlet, he thwarted the attempt of three desperadoes to rob a train at Ponca Station. One of the bandits was Henry Starr. Later, when Starr was on parole from prison and McGeeney directed the filming of his life story, *A Debtor to the Law,* Starr gave McGeeney his Bisley model .45 Colt revolver. For foiling the holdup attempt, the Wells Fargo Express Company presented McGeeney with an 1886 model .38–56 Winchester rifle, and he was appointed the youngest deputy United States marshal for Oklahoma Territory. As deputy marshal, he knew the "greats"—Bill Tilghman, Heck Thomas, and Chris Madsen—and had many other brushes with badmen, including being an eyewitness to the killing of John Wesley Hardin by City Marshal John Selman at El Paso.

From 1906 to 1912, McGeeney served variously as superintendent of construction and roadmaster on the National Railways of Mexico, experiencing numerous hairsbreadth escapes from *bandidos* and the revolutionary armies that overthew President Porfirio Diaz. Establishing himself at San Antonio, Texas, he wrote a dozen novels, more than a hundred articles, plays and scenarios, and operated two photoplay producing companies until 1924. In the interim, he filmed United States troops in action along the U.S.-Mexican border (1916), followed the expeditionary forces of General John J. Pershing into Mexico, and returned to Texas with a fine pair of "star" spurs—a gift from Pancho Villa. In 1919, he traveled thousands of miles through the western United States and into Canada, making a series of documentaries on reservation life of the North American Indian, which the Christian pastor and best-selling novelist, Harold Bell Wright, called a "very valuable contribution to the history of our American people."

Two outstanding McGeeney plays are *St. Patrick's Night* and *In the Penal Days.* Among his books are *Down at Stien's Pass, Down at Cross Timbers, The Power of Love,* and *El Diablo Cojo.* Some of his screen successes are *The Poisoned Pool, The Battle Ground of Nations, Little Dolly Dimples, Little Madcap, Little Miss Bluebonnet, Jim of the 3-C Ranch, Jack of the Diamond A, Perils of the West,* and *The Germ.*

McGeeney loved the Great Southwest, which he described as "a big, undeveloped land of sunshine, peopled with the best and the worst. . .men and women standing clean and true, stripped of the veneer of hypocritical social environment. . .with the hearts of children and souls that respond to the voices of religion like the arrow responds to the string of the bow; loving wisely, hating fiercely, their code becomes their law." Mostly, he loved San Antonio's "quaint charm." With her natural beauty, historical atmosphere, and climatic advantages, he envisioned the Alamo City as a movie capital ranking alongside New York and Los Angeles. Though this ambition was never realized, he flashed the city's beauty around the world and back again; large companies availed themselves of her climate and his studio facilities; and he handled nearly a half-million dollars of eastern capital spent in the production of pictures.

Fortunately, McGeeney preserved much of his career in articles under the pseudonym "Purple Sage" and in a bulky scrapbook of correspondence, newspaper and magazine clippings that detail his hair-raising exploits and pioneer efforts in movie making. These items, with photographs and family memorabilia, were placed at my disposal by his grandson, Thomas Michael McGeeney. I immediately saw a book which offered practically an unknown chapter in American West history. While quoting McGeeney extensively, I have arranged the material into a running narrative and supplied and integrated the necessary historical background and verification.

May the reader enjoy *Purple Sage* as much as I have enjoyed writing it.

Glenn Shirley

Purple Sage

•1 "One Memorable Night"

The time: Mid-spring of 1893. The place: Indian Territory, in full foliage and flower. The event: Henry Starr, notorious train- and bank-robbing bandit, was riding.

Henry was born at Fort Gibson in 1873, the son of a half-Cherokee, George "Hop" Starr, of the old Tom Starr clan, and Mary Scott, a white woman, half-Irish and highly respected. He had grown to manhood in the heyday of the Fort Smith federal district court, when vicious outlaw bands roamed the nations of the Five Civilized Tribes—called "Robbers' Roost" and the "Land of the Six-Shooter." As a teenager, he had felt the disgrace of leg irons of deputy United States marshals on a whiskey charge that he always maintained was uncalled for and that soured him on Judge Isaac Charles Parker's "hanging" justice. At age nineteen, of medium height and strong athletic build, with straight black hair and intelligent black eyes, handsome with just a tinge of swarthiness—his heart and brain throbbing with the desire for revenge—Henry had placed himself in leadership of as scurvy a representation of pariahs as ever infested this outpost of civilization.

In July of 1892, accompanied by a half-blood Delaware Indian tough named Ed Newcome and a lanky, pockmarked whiskey peddler named Jesse Jackson, Starr had looted the Missouri Pacific railway station safe at Nowata and escaped in the Big Caney river country with a purse of $1,700. That summer and fall he robbed safes in the small railroad towns of Lenapah and Sageeyah. In

Henry Starr at Fort Smith, Arkansas, at the time of his conviction and sentence to federal prison for the slaying of U.S. Deputy Marshal Floyd Wilson.

December, he shot and killed Deputy U.S. Marshal Floyd Wilson in the California Creek country and fled west into the Osage Hills. In January of 1893, during a running fight with deputy marshals and Indian police near Bartlesville, Jackson's right arm was shot off and another bullet sent through his body before he was captured. Newcome was captured later at his mother's home near Nowata. Starr escaped, unscathed.

In January, Starr and a Wagoner acquaintance named Frank Cheney robbed two general stores and in February the Missouri, Kansas and Texas (Katy) railway depot at Chouteau of $400, and took $220 from the Missouri Pacific (Iron Mountain) railway depot at Inola. On March 27, with Cheney and five other gang members including a deadly, smooth-faced, hotheaded youngster named Kid Wilson (no relation to the slain marshal), Starr took the Caney Valley National Bank at Caney, Kansas, for $4,900. On May 2, they held up the Katy train at Pryor Creek, obtaining an estimated $6,000 and a consignment of cut diamonds. Cheney and the others sought refuge near Wagoner. Starr returned to his haunts in the Osage.

When and where Henry teamed up with Bill Doolin and George "Bitter Creek" Newcomb is not known. Doolin and Newcomb, former members of the Dalton gang which had met disaster at Coffeyville in October of 1892, were hiding in the Cherokee Outlet between the Arkansas and the Cimarron, following their robbery of the Ford County Bank at Spearville, Kansas. They were launching a new "wild bunch" that was destined to terrorize the recently organized Oklahoma Territory. In mid-May they had been sighted with Starr in the Osage Hills. It was rumored the trio would strike the Santa Fe at some point between the Kansas border and the Oklahoma territorial capital at Guthrie.

Thus the stage was set for Patrick Sylvester McGeeney's opus, "One Memorable Night," which the then nineteen-year-old Santa Fe railway brakeman prepared years later. "On May 19, 1893, at 4:45 P.M., Santa Fe passenger train Number 403 departed from Newton, Kansas, in charge of Conductor A.R. Glazier, with myself as brakeman, flagman Jacob Bender, and Engineer Jules Truslot at the throttle.

"Arriving on time at Arkansas City, the supper station, I went about my usual duties—went to the engine, uncoupled the bell cord, pulled the pin and signaled the engineer to run his engine to the roundhouse, as it was the end of his run.

"On the nearby siding stood Number 97, our regular engine that would pull our train to Purcell [Oklahoma Territory], the end of our division. I threw the switch and let the engine out of the siding to the main line, where I coupled it to the train and connected the bell cord. I then went to the cab and noticed that Jack Regan had replaced our regular engineer, John Rain, at the throttle. The regular fireman also was absent and an extra man sat on the box on the fireman's side of the cab.

"'Hello, Jack!' I called. 'Where's Rain?'

"It was very unusual for Engineer Rain to take a leave of absence and I began to conjure up a great many reasons, for those were the days when almost anything might happen.

"'Hello, kid!' Regan called back. 'Rain and his fireman were in the roundhouse, ready to go, when something important came up. They laid off, and here I am.'

"'Jack, are we going to have trouble tonight?' I asked.

"I could see in his good natured face that he was having the same thoughts that were crowding my mind. But he only shrugged his shoulders.

"Several men were congregated on the platform. Standing apart from the others were C.W. Stockton, Superintendent of the Wells Fargo & Co. Express, with headquarters in Kansas City, and Deputy United States Marshal Heck Thomas, employed by Wells Fargo as a special agent. Both men were heavily armed, holding Winchester rifles in their hands, and talking in whispers. I surmised from their grim faces and actions that perhaps a train holdup was in the offing, and the reason Rain and his fireman had deserted the engine so suddenly.

"'And you, Jack,' I asked, 'are you going to desert too?'

"'Not on your tintype, kid. Still I don't like the idea of stopping bullets. . . . What are you going to do?'

"'The Irish never retreat,' I replied, 'and if I were handling the engine I'd keep my hand on the throttle and my eyes on the track. If I saw anything out of the ordinary ahead, I'd stop the train, whistle three times, wait a few minutes. . . and approach slowly. If all was not well, I'd back up and keep my passengers out of danger.'

"'Good idea, kid. If the occasion arises, I'll do just that.'

"'And, Jack, if the train stops and I hear you toot three times,

I'll come up to the engine and—'

" 'All aboard!' called Conductor Glazier. As the train was passing I grabbed the hand hold, swung onto the steps and entered the smoker.

"It was not my duty, but a task imposed upon me by Conductor Glazier to follow him through the train while he was collecting tickets and see that no harm came to him. During his past life he had made many enemies. Why? His biography has nothing to do with this story. In plain words, I was his bodyguard and I packed a .45 Colt almost as big as I was.

"Stockton and Thomas were seated in the front end of the smoker, and while Glazier was counting his tickets in the sleeper, I took a seat behind them. At sight of me they quit talking, so I contented myself with watching them as they rode in silence. Finally, Stockton consulted his gold hunting case watch, returned it to his pocket, and said to Thomas: 'In a few minutes we'll be at Ponca, and—" He caught my eyes and did not finish the statement.

"So, thought I, Ponca is the place. I wondered where they might have got the information that someone had designs on the train."

What McGeeney did not know was that shortly after the arrival of Number 403 at Arkansas City, Ponca Agent Liddle received word that three suspicious looking riders had been sighted in the Osage a few miles east of the station. Liddle was instructed to be on the lookout. He had telegraphed the word to Arkansas City, and Stockton and Thomas had been ordered to escort the express car. McGeeney continued, "I cannot explain whether it was fear or just a thrill of what might happen at Ponca that came over me. Thoughtlessly I pulled my .45 from the holster and began to inspect it.

"Thomas said: 'Kid, put that thing up. If it should go off the passengers would stampede.'

"Coolly I replied: 'In time of peace prepare for war.'

"He looked long and earnestly into my eyes and read what was on my mind. I smiled at him and slowly reholstered the gun."

Ponca station, thirty miles south of Arkansas City in the Outlet, was a mail and supply drop for the nearby Ponca Agency. Besides a watering tank and stockyards half a mile north, constructed for use of the surrounding ranchers who held grazing rights from the Indians, there was nothing to break the prairie monotony.

Clouds began rolling in from the west shortly after nightfall. A rain was expected. Liddle stepped out on the platform with a lantern, trying to catch a glimpse of the southbound train against the blackening sky. The station pumper, a hanger-on, and two Ponca Agency soldiers were playing cards in the baggage room. At the telegraph window, the agency mail carrier was gossiping with Night Operator Farrell.

Suddenly three bandits appeared on the station platform. Two of them lined up Agent Liddle and the mail carrier with Winchesters. The third shattered the telegraph window with a pistol shot, ordering Farrell and the card players outside. As the headlight of engine Number 97 cut through the darkness, the bandits instructed their seven prisoners to accompany them to the train as protection while they looted the express car.

Inside the smoker, McGeeney felt the weight of the engine against the train. "I knew that Regan had pushed in the throttle and shut off the steam. The grinding of air brakes told me that the train would soon stop. Quickly I left my seat with my lantern in hand, and out the door to the coach platform I hurried as the whistle sounded three short blasts.

"When the train stopped, I jumped to the ground and ran toward the engine. I noticed that the station order board was against us, as its red light indicated. A red lantern was being swung violently by someone standing under the order board. It was a stop anyhow and there was no need for this procedure of signaling."

Then the red lantern disappeared, and all the station was darkness and quiet except for the soft patter of rain. The train had stopped at the stock loading pens. McGeeney hustled up to Regan. " 'Jack,' I exclaimed, 'our hunch is working and it's a good thing for all of us you stopped when you did!'

" 'Yes,' he replied. 'I don't like the complexion of that depot, and—'

" 'Regan!' yelled Glazier, as he hurried up to the engine. 'Why did you stop here?'

" 'Well,' Regan replied, 'this kid told me if I saw anything funny ahead to stop and whistle three times—'

" 'Who the hell is running this train?' interrupted Glazier.

" 'You are,' answered Regan, 'but I'll be damned if I will run this engine into a shower of hot lead.'

"Glazier cooled down when he saw the order board. He seemed to realize we had taken the safe course, but he was loath to admit it.

"Inaction in my young life was a punishment, so I offered a suggestion: 'I'll walk down to the depot, look around, and you'll know the outlaws are there. If you see any signals, you'll know I'm compelled to give them, and that will be your cue to keep the train out of danger.'

" 'Go ahead!' Glazier consented, in a surly tone.

" 'By God, kid, you're brave, but watch your step!' Regan said, as I started away.

"Glazier called me back. 'Kid, take off that Colt and give it to me.'

"I protested.

" 'You're Irish and hotheaded,' Glazier continued. 'You might try to use that gun, and I don't want you killed.'

"This angered me. Was he concerned with my life, or did he want the gun to protect his own? I knew the answer when he buckled the Colt around his waist.

" 'Is it loaded?' he asked.

" 'I don't carry it around to cut my wisdom teeth on!' I snapped back and hurried down the track."

McGeeney leisurely approached the depot, carrying his lantern. Three saddled Government horses—the mounts of the agency soldiers and mail carrier—were tied to iron rings in the planks of the station platform. No one was in sight. He peered in the broken window. The lamp was burning, but the office was empty. He circled the station, tried the double freight door, and found it locked. Slowly he walked toward the water tank. As he passed the end of the high loading ramp, a voice rang out, " 'Hands up!'

"Did my hands go up? Yes, and my lantern with them.

" 'Come this way!' the same voice commanded.

"With a funny feeling in my stomach and weakness in my knees, I advanced, and by the aid of my lantern's light I got a view of three bandits holding the business end of their rifles on seven cowed victims."

McGeeney recognized Henry Starr, Bill Doolin, and Bitter Creek Newcomb. Of course, he was added to their collection.

" 'Why did the train stop?' asked Starr.

"I wasn't as interested in his question as I was watching

and listening to Bill Doolin cocking and uncocking his rifle aimed at my midriff."

McGeeney told Starr the train had stopped because the conductor thought there might be a holdup. Starr asked if there were any armed men on the train besides the express messenger and his guard, and McGeeney replied, " 'Heck Thomas and Charley Stockton, and both are loaded for bear.'

" 'If we get hold of Thomas and Stockton we'll cut their damned throats!' Bitter Creek said . . . I knew old John Barleycorn was speaking.

"Doolin continued his infernal music with the rifle hammer. Should his thumb slip, I'd be strumming a lute in Paradise. . . .

" 'Let me give them a signal to come ahead,' I suggested. 'Perhaps they will come down, then you can get the train.'

"Starr looked at me with a critical eye.

" 'Give the signal,' he said. 'And it had better be the right one!' "

McGeeney stepped a few feet from the shelter of the loading platform. Three times he gave the highball, but there was no response from the train. He knew that Conductor Glazier understood and would act accordingly.

There was an awful stillness among the outlaws. What to do next? McGeeney began to worry about train Number 37, a fast freight that always followed them out of Arkansas City.

" 'Henry,' I said, 'think of the position of those helpless passengers if Number 37, that fast freight which is due in a few minutes, should plow into that train. I know you don't want to kill anybody.'

" 'No, no, by God, we don't!' Starr exclaimed.

" 'Then let us go up and take the train,' I said. 'We've wasted enough time already.'

"Starr hesitated. 'Our horses are behind the stockyards. We can't be left on foot. Boys, get those Government crowbaits at the platform.'

"Quickly Doolin and Bitter Creek obeyed. They returned leading the horses. Doolin handed the reins of one of the mounts to Starr, who hooked them over his arm, then ordered all of us to march toward the train.

"Up the track we were herded. My lantern burned brightly in my elevated hand. The station agent carried one, also the pumper."

McGeeney was convinced that Stockton, Thomas, the express messenger, and his guard realized that train bandits would not make themselves conspicuous by carrying lanterns, and hold their fire as long as they saw the lights. Another thing in the young brakeman's favor was that the close rumbling of thunder and flashes of lightning portended rain at any moment.

"My hopes wilted when Starr commanded us to place our lanterns on the ground along the tall bunch grass that grew in abundance on the prairie. Again I experienced that queer feeling in the pit of my stomach and weakness in my knees.

"Forward we stumbled . . . about two hundred feet . . . parallel with the train. I was edging to one side so that I could make a beeline into the darkness and hide in the tall grass. My attempt to escape quickly died, however. . . .

"I heard a shout from the station: 'Let those men go or we'll blow your brains out!' "

Soldiers at the Ponca Agency had heard the shot that shattered the railway telegraph window. A sergeant and six privates had ridden to the scene to investigate, spotted the bandits with their captives, and were coming up the track.

"Starr turned and roared. I will not write the blasphemous words he uttered. The outlaws jumped into the saddle, put spurs to their mounts, sending a fusillade of shots through the darkness, and disappeared in the direction of the Osage Hills. The soldiers and trainmen all fired at the spot where Starr had yelled his defiance.

"Boy, oh boy! Those bullets zipped and whined over our heads, singing a melody of death to nowhere. In that short moment one sang 'Home Sweet Home' through the bill of my cap, another seemed to whisper 'Nearer My God to Thee!' and still another took a piece of hide and hair from the right side of my head. That little shock vanquished my terror. . . .

" 'Don't shoot!' I yelled. 'The outlaws have gone!'

"I guess the sharpshooters recognized my voice, for the firing ceased. Stockton and Thomas had left the train and come forward to take a hand in the battle. It was my firm conclusion that they had fired the shots that put the fear of God in me. . . .

"Conductor Glazier signaled to go ahead and the train went flying past the depot and vanished around a curve on its way to the bridge that spanned the Salt Fork, leaving Stockton and

Thomas behind. The bandits' horses were captured at the stockyards. We had met with no injury. . . . Lightning illuminated the sky—a clap of thunder and rain began to fall.

" 'Boys,' I called, 'let's get our lanterns and go back to the station.' "

McGeeney sent two telegrams—one to United States Marshal William Grimes at Guthrie, the other to C.B. Strohm, trainmaster at Arkansas City—giving the details of the attempted holdup. Agent Liddle asked, "Where's Farrell?" The night operator had vanished when the shooting began. "We started a search for him and found him 'cooned up' in the rafters of the freight house. Assuring him that the outlaws had gone, we got him down from his perch. He was a pitiful sight from fright.

" 'This is no place for me,' he said, and took off up the tracks to the north. Later I was advised that he had arrived at Arkansas City the next afternoon, having walked the entire distance."

Agent Liddle "opened the key to a call." The message was for McGeeney, who read over his shoulder: "Look out for Stockton and Thomas. . . they were left behind. . . the engineer feared that the outlaws might board the train." It was from Red Rock, the next night station south, and signed "Glazier." But McGeeney "understood the situation." Glazier had "passed the buck" to Regan.

"The agent handed me another telegram from trainmaster Strohm to go to Purcell just in time to return with Conductor Glazier on Number 408, a local passenger train that was due at Newton, the end of our division, at 10:00 P.M. that night. News of the attempted robbery had traveled up and down the line. At every station the usual curiosity seekers plied me with nonsensical questions until I was completely worn out. . . .

"Newton at last! The station was crowded with people. As I stepped from the coach onto the platform, there stood my mother and two sisters. For a breathless moment I gazed into their agitated faces. Then my mother took me into her arms.

" 'My son!' she cried. 'We heard you were dead.'

" 'Why, mother, such nonsense! I'm here. . . very tired and hungry. Let's go home.' "

The next day McGeeney was pestered by reporters wanting a scoop for their papers. He "hated notoriety" and referred them to Glazier. "I do not know what his story was to them. The *Kan-*

The 1886 model .38–56 Winchester rifle presented to McGeeney by Wells Fargo Express Company in 1893. (Insert) Bisley model .45 Colt revolver given McGeeney by Henry Starr, when McGeeney directed the filming of the outlaw's life story, *A Debtor to the Law*.

sas City Journal said: 'Conductor Glazier sent a poor little defenseless unarmed brakeman down to the station, single-handed, to meet the outlaws. . . ." This was far from the truth. Mr. Glazier only accepted my suggestion. . . I went voluntarily, at my own risk."

The Newton *Kansas Republican* carried the "most accurate account," headed with a short poem by "Robin Goodfellow":

Ye're a hero, Pat old feller
An' by gosh hit hain't no fun
Ter be gazin' down the barrel
Of a wicked lookin' gun.

An' the boys are layin' fur ye
An' don't ye never doubt
They'll guy you like the dickens
If you don't watch out.

McGeeney received letters of congratulations from the railway headquarters at Topeka and Wichita, Kansas. For his bravery in thwarting the Starr desperadoes, the Wells Fargo Express Company presented him a Model 1886, .38–56 caliber Winchester rifle. On May 24, at Guthrie, United States Marshal Grimes commissioned him federal deputy for Oklahoma Territory. Grimes' term expired in June. Grover Cleveland had returned to the White House as president in March. Evett Dumas Nix, a Guthrie businessman, became the president's choice for the U.S. marshalship, and Nix recommissioned McGeeney on July 31, 1893.

Henry Starr severed relations with Doolin and Newcomb after the Ponca fiasco. On June 5, he and his old companions—Frank Cheney, Kid Wilson, Hank Watt, Bud Tyler, Link Cumplin, and a dolorous-visaged gunman called "Happy Jack"—rode into northwestern Arkansas, held up the People's Bank at Bentonville, and escaped in a running gun battle, with an estimated $11,000.

The gang divided the loot and decided to split up for a while. They were never reunited. Cumplin died of wounds he received in the Bentonville fight; Watt and Happy Jack were killed in the Cherokee Nation; Tyler died of "natural causes"; and Cheney was slain by deputy U.S. marshals in the Choctaw Nation, near Eagletown. Starr and Wilson fled to Colorado, where they were recognized and captured by Colorado Springs detectives on July 3, 1893.

McGeeney read much about Starr in the months that followed. Starr and Kid Wilson were returned to Fort Smith to answer for their crimes in Indian Territory. They were indicted on fifteen counts and found guilty of six. Wilson received twenty-four years in federal prison. Starr was not sentenced, pending his trial for the slaying of Deputy U.S. Marshal Floyd Wilson in 1892. He was convicted in October of that murder and sentenced to the rope. His attorneys promptly appealed to the United States Supreme Court, which reversed the case on the mitigating circumstances that Starr had killed the deputy marshal in an open fight.

Starr was tried again in 1895, and again convicted and sentenced to die. His attorneys took out a second writ of error, and the Supreme Court ordered a third trial on a technical procedure. Starr remained in the Fort Smith jail until October 1897, when he finally pleaded guilty to manslaughter and was sentenced to three years in the penitentiary at Columbus, Ohio. He drew seven years and seven days on the robbery counts, and five years for the Pryor Creek affair, for a total imprisonment of fifteen years and seven days.

Thus Starr passed from McGeeney's life—temporarily. McGeeney would have future, but far more pleasant, dealings with this most unusual train- and bank-robbing outlaw.

•2
"Delaney's Shadow"

Frontier violence was nothing new to Patrick Sylvester McGeeney. Born near Newtown-Stewart, Tyrone County, Ireland, August 19, 1873, he was little more than a babe in arms when his parents, Michael and Elizabeth "Lizzie" McGeeney, brought him, his older sister Elizabeth Jane, and brothers Edmund L. and Michael, Jr., to America. The family settled at Newton, Harvey County, Kansas. At the time, "Bloody Newton" was still trying to throw off its notoriety as the toughest, loudest, most dangerous shipping railhead for the immense herds of Texas cattle.

Young McGeeney's "Uncle Pat"—his namesake and his father's bachelor twin brother—had come to Newton at the town's inception to engage in the mercantile business, possibly choosing the clime because of its similarity to the McGeeney home on the Emerald Isle. The Atchison, Topeka and Santa Fe Railway officials, who had picked the site in the spring of 1871, had enthusiastically named it for Newton, Massachusetts, home of many Santa Fe stockholders.

The general surface of Harvey County was high grass prairie, rolling to the southeast and drained by the Little Arkansas River, which entered the northwest corner, flowed east a few miles to its confluence with Crooked Creek, then continued southeastward and was joined at various points by Black Kettle, Emma, and Sand creeks. In the eastern part of the county were Jester and West creeks. Bottomland constituted thirty percent of the area, making a fine farming district. Timber belts up to a quarter-mile wide contained a variety of wood—walnut, elm, cottonwood, ash, elm, box elder, mulberry, sycamore, and hackberry. There were limited quantities of magnesian limestone in the northwest and clay of a good quality for brick along Sand Creek; gypsum abounded in the eastern portion and salt in the southeastern section.

Only fifty-some settlers occupied the bounds of the county in 1871. Following announcement that the railroad was coming, Newton sprang into existence almost overnight. The original town plat ran a mile long and a half-mile wide east of Sand Creek. Main Street ran north and south through the center of the tract, and the railroad in a southwesterly direction, crossing Main near Fourth Street. The first building on the site was a blacksmith shop; then came the Newton House, the first of the town's three hotels. Within a few weeks, nearly two hundred residences and frame business places (most of them in the three blocks north of the railroad) had been erected or were under construction. Two public wells—one at the intersection of Fifth and Main, the other at the intersection of Sixth and Main—supplied Newton with "sweet, cold, palatable water." The wooden sidewalks were ten feet wide. The streets were still covered with grass, and after heavy rains, freight wagons plying the stores on Main Street would mire to the axle.

A $10,000 stockyard and a large cottage in which the superintendent resided had been erected a mile and a half west of town by Joseph G. McCoy, who had made Abilene famous as a cattle market. The yards consisted of fifteen subdivisions in which 4,000 head could be confined overnight, six chutes for loading the cattle into shipping cars the next morning, and a Fairbanks scale with a capacity of forty tons. The herds were held on the surrounding prairie, where the grass was rank and green.

By the time the first longhorns, hitherto driven up the Chisholm Trail to Abilene and Ellsworth on the Kansas Pacific, arrived where the iron rails met Newton's sod, the town boasted 1,500 residents—6,000 before the railroad construction gangs departed. An estimated 40,000 head of cattle were shipped out of Newton during the next few months—and the Santa Fe made money. However, eastern capital didn't seem to be interested, and the company's profits fell far short of the estimated five-million-dollar

Patrick "Uncle Pat" McGeeney, early day merchant of Newton, Kansas, was Patrick Sylvester's namesake. "Uncle Pat" later helped found the farming and wool-growing center of Deming, New Mexico.

expense of its grant calling for completion of a settlement-to-settlement road through the territory to the Kansas-Colorado line by March of 1873. It appeared that Newton would be the end of the track for some time. The town boiled with business and sin.

One out of four of the mostly false-fronted buildings facing each side of Main Street was a saloon and gambling house. Harry Lovett opened the first saloon at the northwest corner of Main and Fourth. The Goldroom, the town's most notorious, began doing business shortly afterward on the west side of Main between Fifth and Sixth. Other establishments bore such euphonious names as "The Mint," "The Side Track," "Red Front," "Parlor," "Bull's Head," "Legal Tender," and "Do Drop In." All collaborated in extracting cash from the wild, boisterous, gun-hung youths of the cattle trail.

South of the track, sprawling along Main Street and westward onto the prairie, was Newton's red-light district, suggestively titled "Hide Park." It consisted of several roughly constructed houses, two of which were Perry Tuttle's Dance Hall and the Alamo, kept by E.P. Krum. The other structures were divided into cubicles where "soiled doves" did a thriving business. "Women and ——— are the attraction," wrote a New York *World* correspondent, who visited Newton in August. "They [the dance halls] are but thirty yards apart, and around them the grass is stubbed and yellow. . . dim lanes radiate in every direction. . . worn by the feet of customers [who] are continually crossing from one house to the other to seek. . . a fresh partner."

Fiddle and piano music and the "hippity hop" of dancers dinned at all hours of the night and on Sundays. There were gaming tables in one corner of both Tuttle's place and the Alamo, a bar to accommodate the dancers at the conclusion of each dance, and the ever-present crowd of cowboys, roughs, and casual spectators. A dozen girls were on duty at each hall. "Some," said Judge R.W.P. Muse, who visited Hide Park in its first days, "drank with their male partners, occasionally got drunk, shouted, and swore until a looker-on would have thought that hell had surely broken loose."

A Wichita *Tribune* reporter described Newton as "the fastest town I have ever seen. . . and I have been in a good many. If I had any money, I would not be safe with it here."

Under these conditions, with the attendant gunplay, it was "the wickedest and bloodiest town in Kansas." One early-day resident recalled, "The firing of guns in and around town was so continuous that it reminded one of a Fourth of July celebration from daylight until midnight."

Some of the shooting was in the spirit of amusement, such as "bulleting" the high silk hats of the eastern effete who made the perilous journey west to look the town over. The number of men killed during Newton's one hot and hectic season as a cattle market is not exactly known.

Two Texas cowboys, Snyder and Welch, inaugurated the summer's fatal shoot-outs. On June 16, while they were quenching a three months' thirst built up on the long dusty trek north, some old enmity between them resulted in a quarrel which ended in a revolver duel on Main Street. Welch crippled Snyder, and Snyder killed Welch. Welch became the first occupant of the town's burial spot, "Boot Foot Hill."

A short time later, a mysterious individual named Irwin was gunned down in the Parlor saloon; a young cowboy was shot and killed in a Hide Park dance hall (accidentally, it was claimed); and another unidentified man was killed by being thrown violently from a wagon while drunk.

Newton was still a part of Sumner County in 1871. There was no village or city organization, and the citizens had to rely on the township justices and constable for law enforcement. These officials proved ineffective against the roughs, gamblers, and courtesans who found their nefarious vocations so remunerative and outnumbered the respectable folk five to two. So Uncle Pat McGeeney and other legitimate merchants raised a fund to pay for the services of a night marshal with a deputy sheriff's commission.

Thus the stage was set for the one inglorious episode which became known as Newton's "General Massacre."

The man chosen to keep the peace was Arthur Delaney, who had adopted "Mike McCluskie" as a professional nom de plume. According to Henry Brunner, proprietor of the Santa Fe Hotel, McCluskie was a railroad security agent from St. Louis—a "fine looking, heavy-set, self-reliant Irishman who did not talk much," apparently neither seeking nor avoiding a fight, but "handy with a gun and deadly in his aim." Like most railroaders, he "stood on the side of the homefolks as against the evildoers."

McCluskie was followed on his nightly rounds by a thin-faced, hollow-chested youth named Jim Riley. Riley was only eighteen and suffering the last stages of tuberculosis. No one knew his origin. Settlers moving west on the Santa Fe were, for some reason, called "Zulu." The father or one of the boys rode in a boxcar free, with the farm implements and household goods, while the rest of the family rode in coaches. For a jug of forty-rod the settler got his car coupled just back of the engine where there were fewer jerks, and the brakeman chalked "Zulu-Jug" or "Zulu-No Jug" on the side of the car as a guide to the switchman who made up the train. Jim Riley lay in a Zulu car, ragged, penniless, and half dead, when McCluskie found him. He was beating his way west, he said, in hope of reaching the healthful climate of Colorado.

McCluskie had practically dragged the youth to a doctor to have him treated—which proved fruitless—and provided him with board and some decent clothing. Thereafter, Riley worshipped the burly marshal as if he were the father he couldn't remember. He carried a Colt six-shooter concealed inside his shirt and was willing to risk whatever life he had left for the only man who had ever befriended him. The local toughs likened him to a dog following its master—not in McCluskie's presence, however—and spoke inevitably of the kid's early death.

During his growing-up period in Newton, Patrick Sylvester McGeeney learned much of the town's early history from its pioneer builders including his Uncle Pat. In later years, under his nom de plume, "Purple Sage" (suggested by his P.S. initials), he wrote feature stories about Newton's struggle to become a "clean little city of fifteen thousand souls." In one opus, titled "Delaney's Shadow," McGeeney deals with the McCluskie-Riley relationship.

". . . Delaney and Riley, both good Irish names. Art Delaney had been a construction foreman on the railroad. . . Riley a lunger had drifted in from nowhere. . . . Delaney took a big, brotherly interest in the cough-ridden youth, and Riley took great pride in his self-appointed guardianship. . . . The common phrase used by the townspeople when they appeared upon the street was, 'There comes Delaney and his Shadow.'

"Physically unfit for work, Riley spent his time in the gambling halls. Some days he was flush with money; others he was flat broke. He never boasted of his good luck; neither did he whine when Dame Fortune turned her back upon him. Once when he was a heavy winner Delaney admonished him to give up on Lady Luck and use the money he had won to enter a sanatorium.

"Riley might have taken Delaney's advice had not real trouble for the marshal entered the picture."

On August 11, an election was held to allow citizens to decide if $200,000 in county bonds should be issued the Wichita and Southwestern Railroad Company (a Santa Fe subsidiary made up of local capitalists) for the buiding of a branch line from Newton to Wichita. Free whiskey was set out by the barrel. William Bailey, a Texas gambler and reputed gunfighter, was employed as a special policeman to assist McCluskie at the polls.

Bailey dealt cards at the Red Front saloon and gambling hall. He was a slick dresser, like most of his ilk, and popular with the Texas element, but seldom sober. In his cups, he was overbearing and quarrelsome. As the day progressed so did his degree of intoxication, until he became "thoroughly offensive and officious." In late afternoon, McCluskie remonstrated with him and insisted on finishing at the polls alone. Angrily, Bailey stomped off to the Red Front saloon.

A deep bitterness already existed between the two men. Some latter-day writers insist their enmity originated with a Hide Park girl, over whom they were fierce rivals. McGeeney, in "Delaney's Shadow," cites a "session with the pasteboards," which involved young Riley, a drummer from Kansas City, and a cattleman from Texas. Bailey was dealer.

"The stakes were high. The drummer and cattleman dropped out. Riley and Bailey continued the game. Delaney was standing behind Riley, facing Bailey. The largest pot of the evening was on the table and the two players were ready for the draw.

" 'Cards?' Bailey asked, as his slim white hands fondled the deck.

"Riley strangled a cough. 'Two,' he said.

"Bailey dealt them. 'I'll take three for myself,' he said, with a smile, laying down the balance of the deck.

"Strangling from his coughing and with tears in his eyes, Riley did not see the deal.

" 'Your bet,' Bailey said.

"Riley glanced at his cards. 'Ten,' he said, pushing a stack of chips to the center of the table.

" 'I'll raise you twenty,' Bailey replied.

" 'Here's another fifty,' came from Riley. . . .

"As the youth pushed the chips onto the table, Delaney snatched them up. Riley turned and faced him in surprise. Bailey's wicked black eyes narrowed.

" 'Delaney, what are you doing?' Riley asked.

" 'Me?' Delaney said quietly. 'I'm saving you some money.' His Irish blue eyes looked calmly into Bailey's angry ones. 'Bailey deals from the bottom of the deck.'

" 'You're a damned liar!' Bailey hissed.

"And Delaney drawled: 'You're a crooked thief!'

"Bailey's right hand started to his hip . . . stopped in mid-air. Delaney's hand was already touching the handle of his six-shooter. . . .

"Riley spread his cards on the table. Four kings and a deuce. His pale face flushed with excitement.

"Delaney turned Bailey's cards over—four aces and a jack.

" 'He was set to take you to the hock shop, kid,' Delaney murmured.

"Riley swallowed, hard. 'I'd have bet my life on those four kings. . . .'

"After cashing his chips with the saloon proprietor, he told Delaney: 'I've had enough of gambling for a long, long time.' "

The railroad proposition carried, which called for more celebration. McCluskie began his patrol of the town before dusk. Riley, his ever faithful "shadow," lounged on the street, here and there.

About 8:00 P.M., the marshal dropped into the Red Front saloon. Bailey was there, still drinking. He demanded that the marshal "set 'em up." McCluskie refused, whereupon Bailey, with an oath, assaulted him. Instead of arresting the gambler, McCluskie tossed him onto the sidewalk.

Bailey ran across the street and waited in a hunkered position before the Blue Front clothing store. As McCluskie emerged from the saloon, Riley yelled a warning. Bailey and McCluskie opened fire simultaneously. Bailey's shot missed; McCluskie's ball struck the gambler below the heart. He was carried, dying, to the Santa Fe Hotel nearby and placed in a room upstairs. His lady love from Hide Park, having heard of the tragedy, rushed to his bedside, crying, "Oh, my baby! Oh, my baby!"

Bailey died the morning of August 12. No inquest was held.

It was the unanimous verdict of Newton's permanent residents that the killing was justified and one less gambler would merely help the town's character. When Bailey was buried on Boot Foot Hill, no one offered a prayer at the grave.

The Texas element took the affair seriously. Despite Bailey's drunken bouts and the fact that he had taken money from the trail drivers in card games, he was one of them. The Topeka *Kansas Daily Commonwealth* of August 22 reported, "Sympathy, strengthened by bad counsels, intensified into rage; rage, feeding on itself, verged into revenge; revenge, muttered and whispered, [was] finally outspoken." A small group swore to get McCluskie.

Their leader was Hugh Anderson, a wild and reckless youth who had recently arrived on the Newton prairie with a longhorn herd from his father's ranch in Bell County, Texas. Anderson had been in a couple of gunfights in his home state. Early in June, he had helped the notorious John Wesley Hardin track down and kill Juan Bideno, a Mexican cowboy who had shot to death Billy Cohron, Wes's friend, in a North Cottonwood trail camp near Abilene. Anderson also had been with Hardin later when Hardin allegedly backed down Abilene's city marshal, James Butler "Wild Bill" Hickok. Aiding Anderson in championing Bailey's cause were Jim Wilkerson, a Kentuckian, and William Garrett and Henry Kearnes, both Lone Star men from Anderson's home town of Solado.

In "Delaney's Shadow," McGeeney says that McCluskie was "getting a little shut-eye" at the National Hotel when Jim Riley rushed in with the news:

"'Hugh Anderson and some of his boys are coming into town to smoke you out. Do you know Anderson?'

"'No, but I've heard he is a bad hombre.'

"'He's passed the word that if you don't ride high, wide and handsome [from Newton], he'll give you a dose of lead.'

"Delaney smiled. 'He's bluffing, kid. He wants to see if I'm yellow.'

"'Everybody knows you're no coward,' Riley said. 'But it's no empty threat. Anderson has already started a collection of notches on his gun.'

"For a few moments, Delaney seemed lost in thought. Then, patting Riley on the shoulder, he said:

"'Maybe Anderson needs some time to cool off. . . . I'll go to

St. Louis for a day or two. I've been needing to visit my mother.'"

By the time Anderson and his followers blustered into town, McCluskie and Riley had departed on the afternoon train. This didn't soothe the Texans; they "posted lookouts" and "declared war to the bitter end" should the marshal return.

McCluskie came back to Newton before midnight, Saturday, August 19. "The moon had sought her couch, and the stars alone were nature's watchers," reported the *Daily Commonwealth*. Business in the Main Street saloons and gambling halls was over for the night. "The town was buried in repose, and naught animate was visible save the occasional pedestrian hurrying home or the ghostly outline of a distant horseman returning to his camp." From the low-roofed houses across the track still "twinkled the lights and issued sounds of revelry and mirth." The Alamo had closed. In Tuttle's place, however, the festivities were yet in full swing. "McCluskie was warned that his life was in peril, but thinking himself proof against powder and ball, scorned the warning and went into Tuttle's."

At sight of the marshal, a cowboy at the bar tossed down his drink, ducked outside, and rode hurriedly to Anderson's camp.

It was now past one o'clock Sunday morning. McCluskie was seated at a gambling table in the corner, observing a game of faro and the gyrating dancers. John Martin, a fine young cowboy from Refugio, Texas, who had just come up the trail, treated himself to a good cleanup at the Santa Fe Hotel, and dropped into Tuttle's to join the fun. He sat at an adjoining table and spoke casually to the marshal.

McGeeney writes, "Many in the place were familiar with Delaney and Riley, his shadow, and were surprised now to see Delaney alone. . . . Apparently unnoticed, Riley was leaning against the wall just inside the door, stifling his coughs in a crimson-stained handkerchief. . . his fever-ridden eyes watchful as ever."

Suddenly small groups of patrons began leaving; they had seen the cowboy duck outside and felt it would be smart to be away from Tuttle's. Even the faro players decided they had enough action for the night and departed, leaving McCluskie at the table talking, unknowingly, to one of Anderson's men. Jim Wilkerson kept the marshal distracted, inquiring with feigned curiosity about his road building experiences with the Santa Fe. Garrett and

Kearnes lounged at the bar, eyes roving alternately from McCluskie to the door, awaiting the arrival of their leader. Perry Tuttle realized trouble was afoot and gave the signal for closing. But it was already too late to prevent what the *Daily Commonwealth* called "a carnival of blood."

Anderson entered covertly. Only the Texans noticed him at first. He strode quickly through the dancers and stopped before McCluskie, cocked pistol in hand, and glaring into the widening eyes of the man he had come to kill. His words, beginning hot and hissing, rose to a shriek: "You are a cowardly son-of-a-bitch! I'm going to blow your head off!"

His pistol exploded. The ball ripped into McCluskie's neck and he spun out of his chair. He rose partially to his feet, gun drawn and pointing at his adversary's heart. The cap hung fire. Before the marshal could trigger again, he fell, bleeding profusely, to the floor. Anderson leaned over him and fired a second ball into his back.

As Anderson stood over his victim, pistol still smoking, Garrett, Kearnes, and Wilkerson rushed to his side in arrogant defiance of any possible opposition, and began firing about the room—rapidly and wildly. Terrified dancers, gamblers, and bartenders dived behind whatever shelter was available or streaked for the door. In the melee, a track foreman named Hickey received a flesh wound in the leg, and Patrick Lee, a brakeman, was struck in the abdomen. Nonplussed, John Martin approached Anderson to halt the bloodshed. Martin should have sought shelter like the others, because in the next instant he caught a stray slug in the jugular vein. He staggered from the dance hall to fall dead in front of the Alamo.

In the next minute, from a quarter entirely unexpected, disaster struck the Texans. Posted opposite the dancers, Jim Riley had been unable to warn McCluskie of Anderson's entrance, and had seen his only friend shot down. For a moment, he remained motionless, as if stunned by what was happening. Then the emaciated, supposedly inoffensive youth pulled the Colt six-shooter from among his nondescript garments and poured a withering fire into the startled band of terrorists. Jim Riley fired once, twice, thrice, and yet again and again, the rapid reports detonating like shotgun blasts in the low-ceilinged room, and at each spurt of flame a Texan "bowed to his prowess."

At the sixth shot, somebody hurled a chair at the coal-oil lamp overhead, plunging the room into darkness. Quiet came, "as appalling as had been the noise of death."

After a few long minutes, a nervy bartender reentered the place and lighted a wall lamp. Jim Riley had gone, but strewn on the floor in pools of gore were the victims of his fury.

Hugh Anderson lay beside and almost on top of McCluskie, gasping and groaning, and bleeding from his thigh and leg. Close by lay Kearnes, shot through the lungs, and Garrett, shot in the shoulder and right breast. A few steps away, Wilkerson writhed in agony from a bad wound in his face and nose. Beyond the Texans, huddled among the overturned card tables, track foreman Hickey tried dazedly to stanch the flow of blood from his wound, and Lee, the brakeman, retched horribly in his last agonized moments of life.

Doctor Gaston Boyd, Newton's lone physician, was summoned immediately. By the time he arrived, the dead John Martin had been taken into the Alamo and the dying McCluskie carried upstairs in Tuttle's. Both dance houses were turned into hospitals. Doctor Boyd was "untiring in his professional efforts," and the girls nursed the dying and wounded with "touching assiduity and tenderness."

McCluskie died at eight o'clock that morning. Patrick Lee and Henry Kearnes breathed their last the next day. Lee's body was taken to Topeka; McCluskie and the Texan were buried in Boot Foot Hill. Later, McCluskie's body was removed to Missouri by relatives. Anderson, Garrett, Wilkerson, and Hickey had been moved to a room in the rear of Hoff's general store, north of the tracks, where all except Anderson were reportedly "doing well and will shortly be about."

Coroner Cy Bowman, a well-known pioneer lawyer of Newton, conducted an inquest over the remains of Martin and McCluskie on Sunday, August 20. The jury found that Martin "came to his death at the hands of some person unknown," and McCluskie "by a shot from a pistol in the hands of Hugh Anderson . . . done feloniously and with intent to kill McCluskie." Accordingly, a warrant was issued for Anderson's arrest.

Indignant over the warrant, the Texas crowd talked of burning the town. Newton was in panic over the terrible tragedy and at a loss as how to prevent a repetition. The *Daily Commonwealth* declared it would be "an act of humanity for the military branch of the government to take possession of the town and control it until a civil organization can be formed [with] strength enough to offer protection to its people."

Newton found a solution. Tom Carson, a nephew of the famous frontiersman Kit Carson, had just come down from Abilene, where he had served as deputy under Wild Bill Hickok. Several merchants, gamblers, and saloon keepers quickly held a meeting and raised money among themselves to hire Tom Carson as marshal. The Texans then threatened to kill Carson. Thereupon, a large number of citizens armed themselves with shotguns and revolvers and assisted Carson in patroling the streets. There was no further disturbance.

Anderson remained in the room at Hoff's store, heavily guarded by a group of his friends, who were still spoiling for a fight. Carson and his assistants planned to arrest him, but it was "not deemed advisable. . . as any unusual excitement [due to his condition] would prove fatal." This proved to be "simply a dodge" to get Anderson out of Newton. Between two and three o'clock the morning of August 21, his friends managed to smuggle him aboard a Santa Fe train, hid him in a water closet, and stood guard at the door all the way to Kansas City. There he received medical treatment until able to travel, and was returned to Texas.

Though permanently crippled from the wounds made by Jim Riley's deadly six-shooter, Anderson again ventured up the trail in 1873. In June, at Medicine Lodge, Kansas, he was killed in a hand-to-hand duel with Mike McCluskie's brother, who also lost his life in the fight.

And Jim Riley?

McGeeney concludes, "A search was made for him throughout the town, but no trace could be found. Having avenged the death of the man who had befriended him, he slipped away into the oblivion whence he came.

"It is probable that he soon died of his illness, to this day no one has ever seen or heard of him, but he left as bloody a mark as any gunfighter in the history of the West."

·3
"'Member Me?"

Several violent incidents following the Newton massacre became grist for McGeeney's pen. A large number of horses had been stolen in the vicinity. Shortly after the massacre at Tuttle's, the thief was apprehended at the stockyards and hanged on a wagon pole.

Joseph "Rowdy Joe" Lowe, mustached, portly in a boiled shirt and beaver hat, and his young wife, Katherine "Rowdy Kate," operated a series of bagnios in the Kansas cowtowns and were in Newton the riotous summer of 1871. During one evening of "swilling and gaiety" at Rowdy Joe's, Joe abused Kate. A man named Sweet, from Topeka, threatened to kill Joe and took the drunken Kate to a house nearby. Joe followed to "see about the matter"; Sweet pulled his revolver and Joe "put two bullets into his body." Sweet died three hours later. The killing was held to be "justifiable," but the "Rowdies" soon left Newton under a district court indictment for "maintaining a common bawdy house and brothel." Rowdy Joe was finally shot to death in a saloon brawl at Denver, Colorado.

McGeeney's favorite story, "gleaned from Uncle Pat," involved Daniel Hicks, "a half-breed Indian known as 'Cherokee Dan.'" Hicks was in the habit of getting drunk and shooting up the town—and taking potshots at anybody who interfered with his celebration. On a Saturday night spree, he swaggered into Harry Lovett's saloon and "began perforating an obscene picture on the wall with lead." Lovett, no slouch with a six-shooter, "pumped five bullets into Cherokee." Hicks was buried on Boot Foot Hill.

On August 26, citizens held a mass meeting and adopted an order banning the carrying of dangerous weapons within Newton township. To enforce the edict, Justice of the Peace J.J. Baker doubled as police judge, with Tom Carson acting constable. Captain C.B. King, a veteran of the War Between the States, was commissioned deputy sheriff, and a calaboose "capable of containing any reasonable number" of prisoners was erected. "The few desperadoes who have been in the habit of making their neighbors uncomfortable by a bravo display of pistols and knives, have wisely taken to the prairies," said the *Daily Commonwealth* of August 27. "Judge Muse, who seems to be the head and front of the peace movement, declares that the history of Newton is now to begin afresh."

Nonetheless, flaunting the majesty of the law continued.

At ten o'clock Saturday evening, September 23, Captain King stepped into Tuttle's dance hall and observed one Thomas Edwards in violation of the weapons order. Edwards resisted giving up his pistol. Carson came to King's assistance, his revolver leveled, and with an oath, ordered Edwards to throw up his hands. King took the pistol and Edwards was released. Carson returned to his Main Street patrol. King remained on the dance hall premises.

"Some two hours later," according to the correspondent for the *Daily Commonwealth* of September 28, "King was standing outside the door, in the same fated area which drank the blood. . . of the victims of the Sunday morning horror of a month ago. Edwards approached him and placing a Derringer close to his breast, fired, the ball lodging near the heart. King staggered into the house [and] immediately fell. . . his friends caught him. . . a moment later he was dead. Edwards fled and has not since been seen. . . . The funeral of King took place on Monday, and was largely attended. Business houses generally closed. . . .

"There was no better gentleman. . . in Newton [than] Deputy Sheriff King. Newton is tremendous with excitement and indignation. . . . Cannot Topeka send us a couple of detectives who will do their duty fearlessly and vigilantly? Brute force without sagacity is plenty enough here, but we want men who possess both."

The peace committee, disenchanted with Carson's failure to apprehend Edwards, terminated his services, and Carson returned to Abilene.

In the fall of 1871 agitation to organize a separate county began. At a convention held at Newton in December, a plan for taking ten townships from Sedgwick County, three from McPherson on the north, and three from Marion on the west, was adopted. It was put into effect by an act of the legislature a few weeks later, and the new county was named in honor of James M. Harvey, Kansas' fifth governor. Governor Harvey appointed a complement of county officers, including Cyrus "Cy" Bowman, county attorney; and W.B. Chamberlain, sheriff. These officials were returned to office in the first election of May 1872, and Newton was made the county seat. Newton, organized as a third-class city, elected its first mayor, police judge, and five councilmen. The council, in turn, appointed a clerk; treasurer; city attorney; William Brooks, city marshal; Charles Baumann, a German, as assistant marshal; and J.R. "Jack" Johnston, special policeman.

Brooks had been a buffalo hunter and a stage driver between Newton and Wichita. He was a handsome man, well-built, about forty years of age, and wore his hair, Hickok style, to his shoulders. He carried a Winchester rifle when on duty, and brought it into good use in June of 1872, while attempting to arrest a couple of drunken, pistol-toting trail hands. The Texans fled from Newton, firing at Brooks. One bullet passed through his right breast, two others lodged in his limbs. He chased the pair, sprinkling them with rifle fire whenever in range, and continued the pursuit for ten miles before he returned to Newton to have his wounds dressed. One week later, Brooks resigned to accept employment on the police force at Dodge City, and Jack Johnston became Newton's marshal.

Johnston was a taller and older man than Brooks. He tucked his trouser legs in high-topped boots in the fashion of the period, was fearless, carried a revolver rather than a rifle, and was quick on the draw.

By this time, the town was being freed of its undesirable element. In May of 1872 the Southwestern Railroad reached Wichita, and that town became the stopping point for most of the herds on the Chisholm Trail. The roughs and courtesans moved there, thence to Dodge, as the Santa Fe extended its track westward, leaving Newton with an "off-scouring" of the cattle trade.

One "hangover desperado" was an Irishman named Fitzpatrick,

a fit subject for McGeeney's pen.

At 8:00 A.M., November 7, George Halliday, an Englishman by birth and the township's new justice of the peace, stepped into the Goldroom saloon for his "morning dram." Fitzpatrick approached the judge and asked him to "set up the drinks." Halliday declined, and Fitzpatrick "shot him dead, remarking, 'I've had it in for you, anyway.'" He then pointed his six-shooter at the bartender and demanded "a big glass of liquor," which was served "without quibbles" and "gulped down promptly," whereupon, Fitzpatrick left the saloon.

Word of the killing spread quickly along Main Street. Marshal Johnston was below Fifth Street when he saw Fitzpatrick coming down the sidewalk, reeling, and warbling an Irish ballad. The officer darted into Dave Hamill's hardware store and grabbed Hamill's Winchester, ran up the street to the well, and rested the rifle on the well frame. As the drunken desperado crossed the street opposite the well curb, Johnston called out: "Halt—throw up your hands!" Instead of obeying, Fitzpatrick bellowed like a bull, reached for his six-shooter, and died with a bullet in his forehead.

McGeeney writes, "This was Newton's last affray in connection with the cattle trade. Business became orderly and rather humdrum as the town began a new and steady development."

In 1873 German-speaking Mennonites from Russia began immigrating to Kansas. In 1875 some 400 families, bringing with them two million dollars in gold with which to build homes, settled in Harvey, McPherson, Marion, and Reno counties. The influx continued until nearly fifteen thousand occupied the area. They established their own churches and schools, which offered courses of instruction in both English and German and were a great boost to the economy. The first church was erected at Halstead in 1877. The City of Newton made an offer to have the school moved. Instead, the church founded a new one in Newton, finally opening its doors as Bethel College.

Other school buildings were erected so rapidly that, within ten years, there were sixty-some public schools in the county, and another college—the Evangelical Lutheran (Congregational). Lodges, fraternal organizations, and the Harvey County Agricultural and Mechanical Society were formed early. The first county fair was held at Newton in 1873.

The original McGeeney family residence at Newton, Kansas. Pictured left to right are Elizabeth Jane McGeeney, Patrick Sylvester's sister; Elizabeth "Lizzie" McGeeney, mother; and Mary Winnifred "Mae" McGeeney, sister.

Located midway on the raiload between Wichita and Hutchinson, Newton became the division point of the Atchison, Topeka and Santa Fe, with twenty-four passenger trains daily and a monthly payroll of $85,000. It was proclaimed a city of the second class in 1880. An abundance of natural gas made it a manufacturing center, with grain, alfalfa, and flour mills, a wagon works, cornice works, and threshing machine factory. Business interests included a number of well-appointed stores, four banks, one daily and three weekly newspapers, and a German newspaper, the *Volksblatt*. Among the metropolitan conveniences were two parks, a hospital, library, telephone and telegraph service, waterworks, sewer system, and an electric plant. The town also ranked high as an agricultural center, with three-fourths of Harvey County under cultivation and a farm output averaging three million dollars annually. The county population totaled over 19,000, nearly 7,000 of which resided in Newton.

The McGeeneys contributed their bit to the city's growth. Michael acquired a house and plot of land near the Ash Street Bridge on Sand Creek. He dealt in real estate and operated the ticket office for the Santa Fe until his death in 1892. In 1884 he and Lizzie were blessed with a second daughter, Mary Winnifred, called "Mae.' Most of the McGeeney children were educated in the Newton schools and institutions of higher learning. Michael, Jr., a bachelor like his Uncle Pat, worked as a telegrapher for the Santa Fe and died at Newton in 1911. Edmund found employment as a conductor on the Santa Fe between Dodge City and La Junta, Colorado, where he married and reared a son and daughter. Elizabeth Jane married Charles W. Chapman, a traveling salesman, who family members claimed "traveled on" after she bore him a daughter and a son. She later served as treasurer of Harvey County and would reside in Newton until her death in 1961. Mae married a well-to-do New Yorker, William H. Harrison, bore him a daughter, and died at Elmira in 1957. Uncle Pat McGeeney harkened to the call of the Atchison, Topeka and Santa Fe Company land syndicate in southwestern New Mexico, where he reestablished his mercantile business and helped found the farming and wool-growing center of Deming.

Patrick Sylvester's aspirations were literature and the stage. At age seventeen—temperamental, imaginative, and high-strung—he was scripting plays and trouping with a small stock company through central Kansas. This proved unprofitable. He had "grown up with the Santa Fe"; railroading was "in his blood," and he became a brakeman.

He was always fond of his home town and in later years reminisced in the local papers. One elucidating glimpse, in poetic form, was titled "Newton":

Gee, I wish I was a boy again
In that little Kansas town,
When the old-fashioned times were good
And sledding it was fine.

In memory's eye, I see it still
The doings of yesteryears, and
Those grand old men who made it safe
Wherein good folks could reside.

Such men I never shall forget
Those pioneers so grand,
Who tamed the big wide open space
Into a fairyland.

Ye Gods! I can see them still,
A-sauntering down Main Street
And planning greater things
For the good old Sunflower state.

And I remember our congressman,
Sam Peters was his name.
A darned good man, we need his kind at the present
time
To work out our destinies.

Across the street stands old John Reese,
His red wig slightly awry.
But dog my cats, his pills were strong,
I know to my eternal sorrow.

And old Jim Geary, with his Bill Cody chin,
The Fire Chief was he.
His boots squeaked louder than the boiler shop
Down at the Santa Fe.

There sits old Clark of the Howard House,

Headquarters for the "peddlers."
Two dollars per day was the usual pay,
If you could stand the pressure.

Can you ever forget the butcher boys, Godfrey?
Their steaks were tough and heavy,
'Cause they didn't use a good round square,
They cut 'em on the bias.

And old Ed Marks, the marshal brave,
A pie tin on his chest, strutting 'round.
Bad boys were his hobby,
Caused his frown.

And old Judge Muse of Townclock fame,
But he, poor soul,
Passed away
Before that clock was made.

There was old Joe Gerson, with his clothing store,
And his daughter Becky, a belle was she—
Until young Seymour Heyman threw his rope
And carted her away.

The mighty hunting Swede, Al Swenson...
His dog Cap knew all his birds,
But died before he ever chased a cat.
Poor Cap.

To slight old Cap Bunker
T'would be a dirty shame,
'Cause he fit over and over his battles
In the Arcade's big domain.

Can we forget John Bender of the Santa Fe?
He was a friend to all the kids.
Why? "Tickets," he whistled through his nose.
Thru this he gained his fame.

The Beau Brummel of our day was Cheatam Bill.
A dandy of the upper "Ten," he wasn't short on gab,
For when he spoke, he stuttered,
Then plunked you on the slab.

And Billy May, darn his hide,

He'd squeeze your aching hoofs
Into cowhide, spring side boots
And send you home rejoicing. God ****? bless him.

There was Welsh and Wing, the livery kids,
They had a knack for swapping.
Their daily chow was good hoss meat,
But you never caught them napping.

A little sporting blood we'll now add—
O.B. Hildreth and his famous horse Astrel.
Dan burn my hide, he ran so fast
His legs would buckle under.

And John, his son, rabbit hunting he would go
With a Saint Bernard as graceful as a grizzly.
Now John has quit the rabbits and he's hunting fees—
A lawyer man is he.

Lest we forget old Schuyler Jones
A-loafing 'round with his one-hoss team.
A big man now is Mister Jones
With plenty of filthy lucre.

Frank Dickensheet and his Sand Creek ice,
I never can forget
The tummy aches I did endure
At such a fancy price.

I can see A.B. Gilbert in his bank.
Oh! what a cheerful sight.
With a smile on his face he'd cash your cheque,
Then count you out your "jack."

Remember Cyrus Bowman and his hairy chin,
Grand Marshal of the day,
Mounted on his fiery steed,
Prancing down the way?

His trusty aides strutting behind,
Big fifer Denny, little trap drummer Edwards, And the
man behind the big bass drum,
His name I can't remember
In their wake and out of step,

Hobbled the boys in blue who fit the war
And made the Johnny Reb surrender.

Frock coat, silk topper and heavy cane,
Old Judge Turner ambles down the lane.
And who can say, did he know his law,
Or was he just a plain shyster.

There goes Col. Hoisington of the guards
In uniform so spick and span,
A-stepping mighty purty
And a-leading the band.

His awkward squad a-follerin'
With bull-like roars, his comrades sing,
"Hip...hip...'tention."
He'd make a mighty warrior.

Krehbiel was the blacksmith,
And with his brawny arm,
He'd shoe a hoss, then stop
And listen to your funny yarn.

Ashbaugh was our P.M., faithful he served Uncle Sam.
'Tween times he peddled gossip thru his weekly sheet,
Then flew away to old Eau Claire,
And there he's taken root.

Sam Lehman was a solid man
He cared for nothing soft...
His plows and cultivators stood the test
And were made of good sound stuff.

Old Doc Conrad with his little bag,
A-gallivantin' 'round.
His calls were far and many,
He made them without a frown.

His stalwart sons, Elmer,
Anse, Wier and Kim,
Their duties very heavy
They mastered with a grin.

Last but not least,
His purty little daughter,

Contented not with dad's good name,
She chose to be a Berry.

But—I don't remember—
'Way back in '71
When Delaney and shadow Riley
Helped fill our "Boot Hill" on the prairie.

It happened in Tuttle's, in the bat of an eye,
And with unerring aim,
Some longhorn Texas waddies
Hit the long, long trail.

There, too, our marshal Delaney
Shuffled off this mortal coil,
But Riley vanished into thin air,
Was never heard of more.

While "Newton" dealt with the older generation, McGeeney spoke of his own tribulations in a brief piece titled " 'Member Me?"

"Hi thar, fellers! 'Member me? I wus that little round faced kid with freckles on my upturned nose, big holes in me wee breeks, torn shirt, an' har that stood up straight. A-fishin' on Sand Creek bank wus my only earthly mission.

"When the cats wouldn't bite and the skeeters quit gnawin' on my little red neck, I got downright sad thinkin' 'bout that Uncle Pat of mine. What wus the matter with 'im anyhow? Did the gals give 'im the mitten? or wus they Scotch an' too darned stingy to wed?—that's what I'm thinkin'. T'is sad to repeat. . . I always wanted a gal cousin. You know the kind. . . one who wouldn't take a dare an' tough enough for me to beat up a-practisin' my pugilistic ambitions.

"An' fellers, believe it or not, the saddest part of my young life was a slight. . . when my parents didn't invite me to their weddin'."

•4
"Anyone Can Be A Congressman"

McGeeney had a run-in with three members of the Henry Starr gang several months before his encounter with Starr himself. It occurred at 10:00 P.M. on November 8, 1892, the date that Grover Cleveland was elected to his second term as president of the United States.

As McGeeney recalled in an opus titled "Three Baskets of Grapes," "The night was sultry. . .sky heavily overcast and rain in the atmosphere. Santa Fe passenger train Number 403 pulled out of Arkansas City, the supper station, southward bound [through the Cherokee Outlet] in charge of Conductor Harry Wilcox and brakeman Cal McComb. On this [McGeeney's first] run I was positioned in the unlighted rear end of the half-baggage, half-mail car with a sawed-off shotgun and my Colt .45. We had passed our danger stations—Willow Springs, Ponca and Red Rock—where holdup men were most apt to appear because an escape from any of these places into the Osage Hills could easily be made. At Wharton [a station on Cow Creek, now Perry, Oklahoma] the engine took water and I took leave of my dark and solitary car to ride in the smoker from this point to Guthrie.

"Up the platform I went and put my artillery in the rear of the smoker. There I met McComb and a traveling man named Conway, who was on crutches assisting Old Man Rheumatism to navigate. Then a Britisher wearing a snapped-down cap came from the Pullman to join us.

" 'I say, gentleman, where can I post a letter?' he asked.

"McComb answered: 'In the mail car. No mail box here.'

"Off toward the mail car went Johnny Bull, and a minute later he hurried back, eyes bulging and voice trembling. 'Gentlemen, there is an argument down at the engine and I saw the driver with his dukes up!'

" 'The engineer with his dukes up?' exclaimed McComb. 'I'd better go down and—'

" 'Get back in that car, you bastards!' a voice yelled, then three shots rang out. . . .

"Did we get back in the smoker! Old Man Rheumatism on crutches won the marathon, the Britisher was a good second, and McComb and your Little Brighteyes shared the honor of being third. We hit the front door of the car. . . and were just in time to muzzle a big sandhill piper who was getting ready to make a speech to the passengers about a holdup being staged. We silenced him. . . and he contented himself by sitting on the floor and rubbing his jaw."

A few minutes before Number 403 had arrived at Wharton, a tall, pock-faced stranger armed with a rifle and two six-shooters entered the station, inquired if the train was on time, and purchased a ticket to Guthrie. His actions excited the night operator, who had no opportunity to send a warning. When 403 stopped for water, the bandit stepped onto the platform and began a fusillade to intimidate the train crew and passengers.

Immediately two more masked bandits appeared at the engine, ordered the engineer and Abe Ross, the black fireman, to uncouple the express car and run it and the engine a short distance south to the coal chutes.

McGeeney continues, using the stereotyped black dialect of the time. "The outlaws were cursing Wagner, the express messenger, and John Riehl, the guard, for not opening the express car door. They ordered Abe Ross to batter in the door with a coal pick.

" 'Look heah. . . yo'all, Mr. Wagner and Mr. Riehl. . . don't shoot! Dis am Abe Ross, de fire boy, an' he's got a little wife an' big family to watch-keer ober.'

" 'Hit the door hard, damn you,' one of the outlaws commanded, 'or your wife won't be bothered with her fire boy. Break that door in!'

" 'Please, gentlemen. . . I kain't. Hit am iron!'

" 'Then cut the air and pull the lever. We're moving the express car down the line. We'll *blow* it open!'

"The engine and express car moved slowly down the track. I tried to locate Conductor Wilcox but could not find him. Later I learned that he had locked himself in the *como se llama* [toilet] in the drawing room of the Pullman.

"The coast clear, I went through the cars and found passengers lying flat on the floor and trying to hide under the seats. Outside I went, and stumbled into a man under the station platform. . . quickly drew my Colt and poked him in the bread basket. I thought he might be an outlaw guard left behind to keep the train crew out of the telegraph office. I soon discovered he was the Hungarian boarding car boss under contract with the Santa Fe to feed the track ballasting gang.

"'What are you doing here?' I asked.

"'I just came in from Arkansas City with my meat. I think I've been shot.'

"He was minus his hat and I saw blood running down the back of his head. I took him inside the smoker and bathed his wound with ice water. When he got over his panic, I told him to go back to his bunk car. On the platform we found his packages of meat, and off he went into the darkness through the drizzling rain.

"I made a round of the station, but found no one. It was evident that the night operator had left for parts unknown.

"In the distance, near the [Cow Creek] bridge, I heard an explosion. Some time later I heard the engine puffing and the clicking of wheels over the rail joints. Slowly the express car rolled up to the smoker. Brakeman McComb came from his hiding place, lantern in hand, and gave the signals to the engineer. When the cars were coupled and the engine was pumping air, Conductor Wilcox came from his rendezvous, none the worse for wear.

"The explosion I had heard was dynamite placed by the outlaws on the iron sill of the express car door. The door was shattered. Messenger Wagner and Guard Riehl had given up. . . . The safes containing money and other valuables were time-locked and could only be opened by agents at their destinations. All the outlaws got for their work was Riehl's Winchester rifle, the messenger's shotgun, and three baskets of grapes."

Conductor Wilcox "reported the cause for the delay of his train to the trainmaster at Arkansas City." McGeeney made his report to the U.S. marshal's office at Guthrie. Chief Deputy Marshal

Chris Madsen and a posse were "dispatched to Cow Creek and found tracks of four horses." The bandits had fled in an easterly direction. "The trail at the start was easy to follow because of the recent rain," but was lost at the Arkansas, where the gang had separated and crossed the river into the Osage.

However, the Wharton operator had recognized the pock-faced man who purchased the ticket to Guthrie—Jesse Jackson. By month's end, the pair that attacked the express had been identified as Starr gang members Ed Newcome and a mixed-blood Indian, Scott Bruner. In mid-January 1893, Jackson was badly wounded and captured in a gun battle with deputy marshals near Bartlesville, Cherokee Nation. Bruner also was captured, and Newcome surrendered at his mother's home north of Nowata. At Guthrie, in April, the trio pleaded guilty to a federal indictment and were given two-year terms in the penitentiary. Newcome was taken to Fort Smith, Arkansas, for further trial on prior escapades with Henry Starr in Indian Territory. In exchange for their relatively light sentences, Jackson and Bruner named the fourth participant in the Wharton robbery—Ernest Lewis.

Lewis, a white man "about thirty years old and a dangerous character," was wanted under $1,000 reward for murder in the Chickasaw Nation, and was "the brains," alleged Jackson and Bruner, in the Wharton affair. He had "split" with them over their failure to obtain any money. The Winchester rifle and the shotgun stolen from the express car were in his hotel room at Pawhuska. Armed with a fugitive warrant—which meant bringing in his man upright or horizontally—Deputy Marshal Heck Thomas proceeded to the Osage country, captured Lewis, and recovered the weapons. When arrested, Lewis was "heavily armed with two revolvers and a big dirk knife."

McGeeney notes, "None of the bandits ever told what happened to the three baskets of grapes."

When Thomas delivered his badman at Guthrie, the new territorial jail housed a large number of prisoners. Some sections were yet to be completed, and it was decided to take no chances with such a desperate man as Lewis. He was transferred to the county jail at Oklahoma City, and was awaiting trial in May 1893 when McGeeney thwarted the attempt of Henry Starr, *et al,* to rob the Santa Fe train at Ponca station.

In jail, Lewis became acquainted with Flora Quick Mundis,

a rather prepossessing young female horsethief, who represented herself as a Cherokee half-blood, dressed in men's clothing, and operated under the alias Tom King. Tom was being held for numerous thefts in Oklahoma, Logan, and Canadian counties. Lewis painted her a rosy picture of the opportunities in train robbing. At three o'clock the morning of June 27, she displayed her charms to a none too bright turnkey, locked him in her cell, and escaped with Lewis. By June 29, they were camped in the Outlet, waiting to rob the northbound Santa Fe train as it crossed the Black Bear Creek bridge between Wharton and Red Rock. To assist in this endeavor, they engaged an acquaintance of Tom King's, a farm youth of questionable mentality, named Immanuel "Manuel" Herrick.

Contemporary reports described Manuel as "seventeen years old, with not even a pinfeather sign of whiskers. . . . He is quite good-sized, a narrow forehead, and small eyes set close together." A native of Ohio, he had migrated with his parents, John and Balinda Herrick, to Greenwood County, Kansas, in 1877, thence to Oklahoma Territory about 1891, settling in Cleveland County, near Norman. He had received little formal education, but was an avid reader of James Boys stories, detective novels, the Bible, and Blackstone—a "self-made man," he told farmers for whom he did odd jobs in Cleveland and Oklahoma counties.

On June 21, six days before Lewis and King's jailbreak, Manuel was found to be insane but not a fit subject for institutional treatment and confinement. He was returned to the care of his father. Where and how he met Tom King is not known. He had been in the custody of Oklahoma County authorities pending his hearing. It was later believed that he had furnished the horses on which King and Lewis made their getaway.

In any event, Manuel boarded Santa Fe train Number 408 at Norman, at 3:30 P.M. on June 29, dressed in a dirty old coat, heavy boots, and overalls and carrying a long, bulky package which he placed at his feet in the smoking car. Near Guthrie, Conductor Al Glazier noticed that the red passenger ticket he had placed on the youth's shabby black hat was missing, and asked him what had become of it. Manuel said he did not know. Glazier found the ticket on the floor and replaced it, telling him not to drop it again. He saw no more of the youth and his package after

Number 408 left Wharton, and thought he had gotten off the train.

All of this became the basis for McGeeney's sequel to "Three Baskets of Grapes," entitled "Anyone Can Be A Congressman": "The little teakettle, nobly pulling its long train of five cars, went panting and puffing up a slight grade and around some curves. Conductor Glazier had settled himself comfortably in the front seat of the smoker, and through his goggles was taking a bird's-eye view of the Wichita *Eagle*. Andy Payne, route agent for the Wells Fargo Express Co., and your fearless marshal—believe it or not, I was the youngest deputy United States marshal ever appointed—were lounging in the coach behind the smoker, with our dogs propped up on the seat in front of us. The bridge over Black Bear Creek was undergoing repairs and was stilted up on jacks. A standing order had been issued to all trains to pass over it slowly. . . .

"As the train began slowing down, Joe Murphy, the handsome news butch, came from the rear of our car. He stopped to gab with us, then started to enter the smoker with his basket of peanuts and catch-pennies on his arm. Something he saw caused him to turn suddenly.

"Curiosity always kills the cat, so I jumped from my seat and we met head-on in the aisle. There is no need to say the peanut market took a sudden slump. What he saw and what I observed was Conductor Glazier with his dukes clawing air, and right behind him a bold bad hombre with a rifle in his hands, rattling a bone solo on poor old Al's ribs."

After the train crossed the bridge, Manuel Herrick had come out of the water-closet with a six-shooter and a Knights of Pythias sword buckled to his waist and a Winchester in his hands. He covered Glazier with the rifle and ordered him to "Stick 'em up!" which the latter did. His next order was "Pull the bell cord." Again the conductor complied. When the train stopped, Herrick commanded him to get off the car.

McGeeney continues: "I flew back through the car and into the Pullman. . . . Afraid? Not I! I craved excitement . . . and was about to satisfy my hunger. Grabbing my rifle, I sallied forth to do battle.

"Out of the Pullman and past the chair car I gumshoed. Glazier came down the front steps of the car I had vacated, while the bold bad man descended from the rear steps of the smoker. His dismal chant reached my beautiful batwing ears: 'March up to the engine and call down the engineer and fireman!' "

As Glazier started forward, Herrick tripped on his sword, throwing him off guard momentarily. Glazier grabbed the rifle and wrenched it from his grasp with one hand, and struck him across the face with the other. "The rifle exploded. . . the bullet went up into the air. Then the bad boy tried to make his getaway. . . . Glazier started after him, but his neat wee feet became entangled in some bunch grass, and down he went like a ton of coal.

"Now was my chance to hog the scene! Throwing the stock of my beautiful .38–56 to my hip, I covered the bad boy, who was struggling to unholster his six-shooter.

" 'Hands up, you buzzard, or I'll give you a dose of lead!' I roared.

"That got his 'nanny.' Up went his bread hooks, and in a trembling voice he pleaded, 'Mister, don't shoot me.'

"By that time Al was at my side, and I said: 'Watch him, Al.' Glazier pumped a fresh cartridge into the barrel of the bad boy's Winchester.

"Behind the outlaw I went and frisked him. Besides the .45 Colt [and sword], his assortment of teeth consisted of two sticks of dynamite, some fuse, a small bottle of coal oil, and a large box of matches. From garret to cellar I rummaged to be sure he hadn't hidden the joker out of the deck.

"Meanwhile, Andy Payne had secured a pump shotgun and was hunting around for more badmen. Andy was brave. Was he! We found out afterwards that his shotgun wasn't loaded. Eagle-eyed Andy spotted a man huddled on top of the express car and ordered him down. As we lined him up beside the bad man I had captured, I burst out laughing. It was Mike Costello, a lad from my old home town. . . . An old Dunkard with a flat hat and hooks and eyes festooning his coat joined us. Was he agitated! The doormat under his chin was smoking. He was in the chair car when the holdup man appeared and had chucked his wallet out the window.

"I escorted my prisoner into the express car for safe keeping. . . . Up in a cut the railroad passed through I saw two riders leading an extra horse. I fired two shots at them, and they galloped madly down a draw.

"When the train pulled out, the Dunkard was left behind, still searching for his wallet.

"I asked my prisoner what he intended to do with the dynamite and coal oil.

"He said: 'That was to blow up the track in front and behind the train.'

"He clammed up when I asked who his companions were."

At Red Rock, Glazier telegraphed a report to the U.S. marshal's office, and asked, "What shall I do with him? I think I had better take him to Wichita."

Chris Madsen and a posse hurried to Black Bear Creek by special train, but "could do nothing except look around." They found tracks and other signs where a man and a woman had been camped near the railroad and decided it had been Lewis and Tom King. Heck Thomas went to Wichita and returned Manuel Herrick to Oklahoma.

Herrick was arraigned on an attempted robbery charge before U.S. Commissioner Bowles, June 30, 1893. The *Daily Oklahoma State Capital* reported, "He looked foolish, but when started on the story of his deed, [became] rather loud-voiced, and in his ignorant way. . .essayed to demand all that he thought should be given to a case of his importance." He declared that he had been "bullet ordered" by members of the recently formed "Bill Doolin outlaw gang," whom he had met while working on a farm at Ten Mile Flats, near Norman, and had "boarded the train to perform the part assigned him." Judge Bowles placed Herrick under a $1,000 bond and ordered him held in the U.S. jail. Authorities found no credence in his tale, and in light of his sanity hearing of June 21, he was committed to the Oak Lawn Retreat at Jacksonville, Illinois, where Oklahoma Territory farmed out its mentally ill.

Did McGeeney receive a reward? "Not so you could notice it. The Wells Fargo gave Al Glazier three hundred bucks for his bravery, and he spent the money to take his family to the World's Fair in Chicago. I didn't begrudge him that pleasure, as Al was a hard working man."

Tom King parted company with Lewis after the Black Bear Creek affair and went back to stealing horses. She was arrested in Canadian County, again escaped jail by tricking the turnkey, and finally left the territory. She allegedly was killed in a holdup near Tombstone, Arizona. Lewis fled to Colorado, thence to Oregon, and finally returned to Bartlesville, Oklahoma, where he was slain in a gunfight with two deputy U.S. marshals on November 18, 1907.

Of Manuel Herrick, McGeeney says, "Days and months rolled into years. From time to time there flashed on the front pages of great newspapers bold headlines concerning an eccentric Congressman from Oklahoma—'Herrick Sued By His Stenographer For One Hundred Thousand Dollars,' 'Herrick Rides in An Airplane,' etc., etc. I couldn't help following the crazy doings of this bold bad boy I had captured at Black Bear bridge."

After a brief stay at Oak Lawn Retreat, Manuel had rejoined his parents on a claim they had obtained seven miles southeast of Perry, in Noble County, following the opening of the Cherokee Outlet to settlement in September of 1893. He was now extremely strong, weighing almost two hundred pounds. He continued to read the Bible, and regarded himself as a great preacher. He preached for hours in his backyard, forcefully and in a high-pitched voice that could be heard for some distance by his neighbors. He also spent much time caring for his numerous pigeons, cats, and other pets, and hunting with wolf hounds.

He was never popular in Noble County, but liked to see his name in newspapers, and soon after statehood in 1907, ran unsuccessfully for county sheriff, county commissioner, and other public offices. Though current Oklahoma laws require a restoration of competency by the courts, in those days it was assumed that all former rights reverted to an individual when released from a mental institution. In 1920, Herrick went around boasting that he would be the next congressman from Oklahoma's Eighth District.

McGeeney explains, "It was a standing joke, and some of the wags put up the money and had his name printed on the ballot. In the runoff he was snowed under, but just before the general election the Republican incumbent died, so Herrick's name was put on the ballot and the Republicans (how they hated to do it) snowed the Democrat under."

Herrick's service in Washington from March 1921 to March 1923 was undistinguished and embarrassing to his constituents: "He was sued for $50,000 by the guardian of a New York girl, and later sued by his Oklahoma stenographer for breach of promise. Following his political defeat, he charged members of Congress drank openly and 'the smell of liquor on all sides sickened me.' Ironically, a short time afterwards, he was arrested with two other men. . . operating a 10,000-gallon capacity still in southern Maryland, and sentenced in federal court to six months in jail.

"I wonder that anyone can be a Congressman."

His parents deceased, Herrick returned to the family farm in Noble County. In the mid-1930s, like thousands of other Depression ridden Oklahomans, he migrated to California. There he attempted several enterprises, but his fortunes continued downward. A blind pensioner in 1952, he lived on a mining claim near Quincy, in the northern part of the state, where, in February, a search party found his frozen body during a snowstorm.

•5
"John Selman"

The Doolin gang that Manuel Herrick claimed had "bullet ordered" him into the Black Bear episode consisted of Bill Doolin; his sidekick Bitter Creek Newcomb; William Marion "Bill" Dalton, whose brothers had met their fate in October of 1892, at Coffeyville; William "Tulsa Jack" Blake, a cowboy-gambler; Charles "Dynamite Dick" Clifton, a Chickasaw Nation whiskey peddler, who filled the leaden points of his cartridges with dynamite to give them explosive as well as striking power; Roy Daugherty, a Texas cowboy who hailed from Doolin's native state of Arkansas and went under the alias "Arkansas Tom"; and George "Red Buck" Waightman, a Texas horse thief whose nickname derived from his deep red hair and mustache, surly disposition, and reputation as a killer. On June 11, 1893, Doolin, Dalton, Newcomb, Tulsa Jack, and Dynamite Dick held up the Santa Fe's Southern California and New Mexico Express No. 3 a half-mile west of Cimarron, Kansas. They secured several hundred dollars in silver from the way safe and fled back to Oklahoma Territory. The last week in August, the U.S. marshal's office learned that the outlaws were rendezvoused at Ingalls, an isolated farming community thirty-five miles northeast of Guthrie and ten miles east of Stillwater, in Payne County.

Since taking over the duties of U.S. marshal on July 1, E.D. Nix had been too busy organizing his new force of deputies to give serious pursuit to the Doolin bunch. He also had been shouldered with the responsibility of policing the Cherokee Outlet. Long coveted by would-be white settlers, the Outlet was an empire of six million acres stretching sixty miles south from the Kansas border. President Cleveland suddenly had proclaimed it would be opened to settlement at high noon on September 16.

Nix had sent most of his regular deputies to the several border registration booths, where thousands of people were compelled to file their intentions and qualifications for the right of homestead entry, and to Wharton, Enid, Alva, and Woodward—railroad townsites destined to become boom cities. His chief deputy, John M. Hale, was attending a term of court at Stillwater. Nix himself had gone to Orlando, on the southern border of the Outlet, leaving Deputies Heck Thomas and John Hixon (a former Logan County sheriff) in charge at Guthrie.

Hixon decided to lead a large posse against the Doolins at Ingalls on September 1. His idea was to enter the town in two covered wagons—one from Guthrie, one from Stillwater—each with a single driver and a squad of six officers with arms and ammunition carefully concealed beneath their canvas. Everywhere homeseekers were crossing the territory bound for the Outlet, so the wagons should attract little or no attention. Heck Thomas considered it a "fool's errand" and elected to remain at Guthrie to handle any emergencies.

Quietly, Hixon rounded up thirteen possemen. About half were township constables and city marshals carrying U.S. deputy commissions. The fourteenth member of the expedition was to have been Patrick Sylvester McGeeney: "Sheriff Hixon met me [the morning of August 31] as I was coming down the steps of the Federal jail where I had gone to identify some bad boys lodged there who were supposed to be train robbers.

" 'Kid,' he said, 'I've organized a posse and I want you to go with us to Ingalls after the Doolin gang.'

" 'Sure,' I readily agreed. 'When do we start?'

" 'Right after dinner. Where will we find you?'

" 'I'll be waiting at the Hotel Royal.'

"Strolling back to the hotel, I met Ada Hixon, the sheriff's daughter, and the Santa Fe roadmaster's daughter, Minnie Brown. . . charming young ladies with whom I had a friendly acquaintance. They asked how long I would be in town. I confided that I was going with Sheriff Hixon after the Doolin outlaws. They

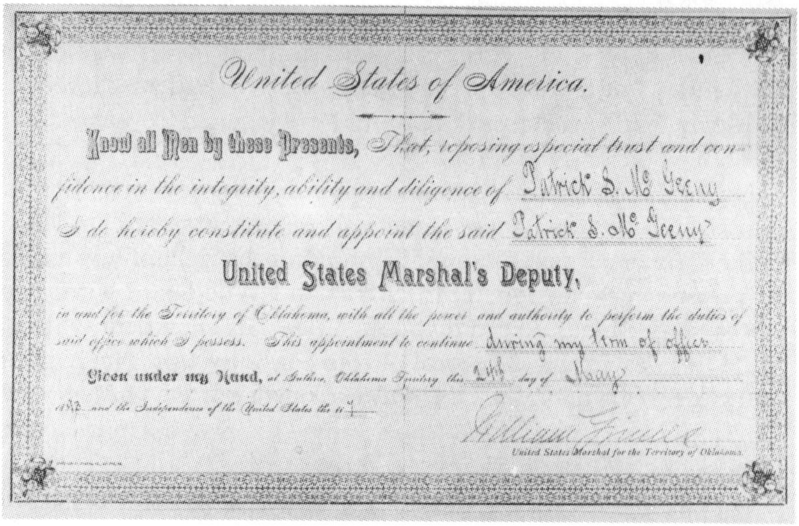
United States of America.

Know all Men by these Presents, That, reposing especial trust and confidence in the integrity, ability and diligence of Patrick S. McGeeny

I do hereby constitute and appoint the said Patrick S. McGeeny

United States Marshal's Deputy,

in and for the Territory of Oklahoma, with all the power and authority to perform the duties of said office which I possess. This appointment to continue during my term of office

Given under my Hand, at Guthrie, Oklahoma Territory this 24th day of May 1893 and the Independence of the United States the 117

William Grimes

United States Marshal for the Territory of Oklahoma.

U.S. deputy marshal's commission issued to McGeeney by United States Marshal William C. Grimes, at Guthrie, Oklahoma Territory, May 24, 1893.

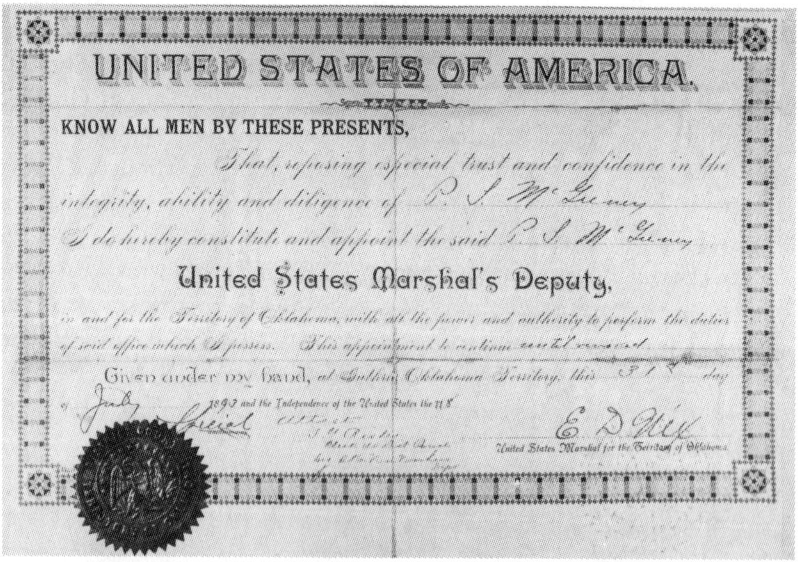
UNITED STATES OF AMERICA.

KNOW ALL MEN BY THESE PRESENTS,

That, reposing especial trust and confidence in the integrity, ability and diligence of P. S. McGeeny

I do hereby constitute and appoint the said P. S. McGeeny

United States Marshal's Deputy,

in and for the Territory of Oklahoma, with all the power and authority to perform the duties of said office which I possess. This appointment to continue until revoked.

Given under my hand, at Guthrie, Oklahoma Territory, this 31st day of July 1893 and the Independence of the United States the 118

E. D. Nix

United States Marshal for the Territory of Oklahoma

U.S. deputy marshal's commission issued to McGeeney by United States Marshal E.D. Nix, July 31, 1893.

tried to prevail on me not to go, but I would not listen.

"My noonday meal over, I went into the hotel office where I saw Governor [William O.] Renfrow in close conference with Miss Hixon and Miss Brown. They ignored my presence, and in a few minutes a white-topped wagon stopped in front of the hotel. Sheriff Hixon alighted and entered the office.

"There was a sharp exchange of conversation, Hixon arguing, 'Governor, he's a deputy United States marshal and can join me if he chooses to do so.'

"Renfrow replied: 'And I am Governor of the Territory. Although this young man holds a very responsible position with the Santa Fe and has done exemplary duty in protecting its trains and identifying Federal prisoners, he is a minor, and I forbid you to take him on this manhunt. He might return in a little box.'

"The sheriff eyed me for a moment, not sure that I would accept the verdict. 'Kid,' he said, 'I'm sorry you can't be with us to see the fun.'

"His daughter kissed him on the cheek. He shook hands with the Governor, Miss Brown and me. Out of the hotel he hurried, jumped into the wagon and drove away.

"I was sorely disappointed and told His Royal Highness that he had no right to prevent me from joining the posse. The Governor only shook his head and smiled. Then he left the hotel—and me to the mercies of the ladies.

"Yes, both of them told me I should be grateful, and left me to do penance for my transgressions."

Afterwards, McGeeney thanked the two ladies—and his lucky star. "The outlaws were warned of the posse's coming, and when Hixon and his men drove into Ingalls the morning of September 1 they were met by a fusillade of hot bullets. During the battle Deputies [Lafe] Shadley, [Dick] Speed and [Tom] Hueston and two citizens were killed, and two outlaws wounded. . . . A lone rifleman, Arkansas Tom, who was hidden on the second floor of the hotel, helped the gang escape. He surrendered. . . was brought to Guthrie, then taken to Stillwater for trial. Judge Frank Dale of the Federal court sentenced him to fifty years in the penitentiary."*

* For a detailed account of the Ingalls fight *see* Glenn Shirley, *West of Hell's Fringe*, University of Oklahoma Press, Norman, 1978, pp. 149–166.

The Ingalls battle was one of the bloodiest ever fought between lawmen and organized banditry on the frontier. But it was the beginning of the end for the Doolin bunch. Over the next two years they were hunted down, singly and in pairs—either slain or given long terms in prison. Doolin himself was captured at Eureka Springs, Arkansas, in January of 1896, by the famed border lawman William Matthew "Bill" Tilghman. In July, while incarcerated at Guthrie awaiting trial, he engineered a wholesale jailbreak. In August, he came from hiding to smuggle his wife and son into New Mexico. Heck Thomas and a posse met him on the trail. He declined to surrender, and was riddled with buckshot.

McGeeney continued his work with the Santa Fe. He came to know intimately the most active manhunters of the day—Thomas, Tilghman, Madsen, and Charles F. Colcord (a former sheriff of Oklahoma County and long-time deputy U.S. marshal in charge of the Fourth Judicial District at Perry after the opening of the Outlet)—and he wrote biographical sketches of these men and their exploits. These articles present the well-known facts (and some folklore), which need not be repeated here. In a rather lengthy opus on Tilghman, titled "Handsome Bill," McGeeney tells how Tilghman, as Perry's first chief of police (1893–1894), tamed the boom town's sinful section called "Hell's Half Acre." He notes one Hell's Half Acre character, a gambler called "Three-Fingered Jack," with whom he became involved personally. "I had known him in Arkansas City and Guthrie, where he plied his trade about two years before coming to Perry. His real name was J.L. Patterson. . .from West Virginia. Two digits were missing from his left hand. He worked as a dealer in Raushman's gaming house."

In a brawl with two strangers the evening of September 26, 1893, Jack was shot through the hip and body. The strangers "beat a hasty retreat and escaped from Perry in the darkness." The wounded man "lost a lot of blood" and was "out of mind" by the time a doctor examined him. The doctor stated that he "could not live more than a few hours," and it was imperative that his identity be established "so his next of kin could be notified." Raushman, however, insisted that he be rushed by train to the Emerson Sanatorium at Winfield, Kansas.

"Santa Fe passenger train No. 406 had just arrived in Perry.

I saw the wounded man when the Noble County sheriff [J.C.] Scruggs and his deputy put him on a cot in the baggage car.

"I rushed up the steps to the platform, and as I passed through the doorway a voice called out:

"'I wish I had my gun!'

"It sounded like the voice of a raving drunk. . . . As I approached the cot, fire flashed from the man's eyes, and he again called out:

"'I wish I had my gun!'

"Then I realized he was addressing me. . . thinking I was one of the strangers who had shot him.

"Yes, I knew J.L. Patterson. . . told the sheriff he was from Bedford County, West Virginia.

"He tried to rise from the cot and the deputy gently held him down. 'Jack,' he said, 'you're mistaken. This is not one of the men who shot you.'

"'You're a damned liar! Get me a gun and I'll kill him!'

"My presence agitated the pain-crazed gambler and I quietly left the car. . . . The conductor called 'All on board!' and the train pulled out."

The attempt to save Patterson's life was in vain. "He passed in his checks at Dr. Emerson's hospital shortly after midnight. . . . Mr. Raushman's efforts to contact friends or relatives failed. The body was buried that evening in the Union Cemetery. . . . Mr. Raushman paid all the funeral expenses."

In 1895 McGeeney became an "undercover man" for the Santa Fe and Wells Fargo Express. "It was my duty to ride the night passenger trains from Newton and Arkansas City to Guthrie and Purcell, Oklahoma, to help protect them from the outlaws. . . . Guarding trains every night was a tiresome job. On the first of August, I asked for a two-weeks rest."

McGeeney was in Guthrie when the approval came through. Dropping by the marshal's office to announce the news, he told Chief Deputy Hale, "'I will leave Newton on the first train, then on to Deming, New Mexico, to pow-wow with my Uncle Pat. On my return I will stop at El Paso, and will cross the Rio Grande to Juarez and make the taverns roar.'

"'Kid, never mind making the taverns roar,' Hale said. 'There is a prisoner in El Paso who is wanted here.' From a pigeon-hole in his desk he handed me a long envelope. 'Take these papers to the United States Marshal at El Paso. They are your authority to bring the prisoner to Oklahoma. He is a bad hombre—don't let him escape.'

" 'I'll bring him in right side up and plant him in the Guthrie *juzgado,*' I promised, proud that Mr. Hale had confidence in me. I bade him farewell. . . . The Santa Fe gave me transportation to Deming, El Paso and return. When I boarded the train [at Newton] I heaved a sigh of relief."

McGeeney provides no detail of his visit with Uncle Pat. Apparently he departed Deming on Friday, August 16, for he spent "three days" sightseeing in Juarez before recrossing the border to El Paso the evening of August 19. "I shall always remember that date. It was my [twenty-second] birthday. . . the night that the threats and hard feelings between the old constable John Selman and the notorious John Wesley Hardin reached a climax."

In a sketch titled "John Selman," McGeeney writes, "There are two killer types of western gunmen. One, the brave man, will give his opponent a fifty-fifty break and kills only in self defense. The other, who always sees red without provocation, will neither give odds nor fight fair. Too, the see-red killer class are always jealous of each other and proud of the number of notches that adorn the handles of their Colts. They consider it a signal honor to send over the Great Divide one of their number who has more killings to his credit than his executioner. To the latter type John Selman belongs. He was a rover and his dessert was strife and gunpowder smoke. Perhaps his experience as a Confederate soldier had case-hardened his heart and poisoned his instincts toward his fellow man."

McGeeney summarizes Selman's career from his birth at Madisonville, Arkansas, in 1839, through his military service and post-war exploits as farmer, rancher, saloon owner, cattle rustler, and deputy sheriff in New Mexico and Texas until the late 1880s, when he moved to wide-open El Paso and became constable of El Paso's First District—the office to which he was to be reelected the remainder of his life. One of his first acts as constable was the killing of Baz Outlaw, who killed Texas Ranger Joe McKidrict. In this battle, Selman was shot in the leg, which caused him to use a cane and limp. By 1895, he was pushing sixty, with more than twenty killings to his credit, and subject to becoming a notch on some jealous gunfighter's pistol butt. His son, John Selman, Jr., was employed as an El Paso policeman.

McGeeney does not mention Hardin's lifetime of homicidal activity and the estimated forty victims he left behind; nor does he note the sixteen years he spent at hard labor in the Texas state prison at Huntsville, where he also studied law. Pardoned in 1894, he was admitted to the Texas bar and hung up his shingle briefly at Gonzales before transferring his practice to El Paso. One of his first clients at El Paso was a bosomy, blue-eyed blonde and former prostitute, Helen Beulah Morose. Her husband, Martin Morose, was hiding in Juarez with a $1,000 reward on his head for cattle stealing, and she wanted him kept out of the hands of El Paso lawmen and returned to home comforts. After one look at the luscious Helen Beulah. Hardin took the case and was soon providing her the "home comforts" she desired. Wild with jealousy, Morose attempted to cross the Rio Grande the night of June 21, 1895, in the hope of killing Hardin. He was met on the Mexican Central Railway bridge by Deputy U.S. Marshals Jeff Milton and George Scarborough and Texas Ranger Frank McMahon, and slain in a wild barrage of gunfire.

The part played by John Selman and his policeman son in the affair is not known. It was believed they had informed Martin Morose of his wife's and Hardin's clandestine relationship as a way of luring him across the river. On August 2, while Hardin was absent on business in New Mexico, Helen Beulah appeared on the street drunk and disorderly and challenged John Selman, Jr., to a shooting match, without specifying the target. Policeman Selman arrested her for carrying a pistol, for which she was fined $50.

Upon returning to El Paso, says McGeeney, ". . . the infuriated Hardin fiercely berated Old John for siring a son 'that's a bastard'. . . who wouldn't have 'robbed and insulted' his blonde *mejur* had he not been away.

"Old John told Hardin: 'You son-of-a-bitch, there is no man on earth who can talk about my boy like that!'

"Hardin said: 'I am unarmed.'

"Selman said: 'Go and get your gun. I am armed!'

"Then Hardin said: 'I'll get my gun and when I meet you I'll meet you smoking.'"

After supper, August 19, McGeeney "strolled around to see

El Paso by candlelight." The night was "sultry, with heavy humidity." He was scheduled to depart early next morning with his prisoner for Oklahoma. As the hour grew late, he stopped at the Acme Saloon "for a last glass of beer." He noticed John Selman "sitting in front of the saloon on a beer keg," talking with his son and M.E. Ward, a railroad man. McGeeney exchanged greetings with Ward. Ward crossed over to the Oxford Saloon as McGeeney entered the Acme. "While I was sipping my beer, I listened to two old cattlemen seated at a table near me relating their adventures. Their stories centered around Cochise, Geronimo, John Ringo, Pat Garrett, Billy the Kid, and other border characters. Hardin, wearing a black frock coat and string tie, and another man [a grocer named Henry Brown] stood at [the] end of the bar next to the door, rolling dice at 25 cents a throw.

"'Hoss piss on you,' Hardin said.

"'Shake again,' the other man replied, and they continued their game.

"The hands of the clock on the wall were stealing past 11 P.M. I was about to bid the two cattlemen good night, when the swinging doors opened cautiously and John Selman limped in. Every patron in the place quit talking. . . the only sound came from the dice as they rolled over the bar, and Hardin remarked: 'You have four sixes to beat.'

"Without warning, Selman fired his six-shooter. Hardin toppled and fell. . . . Three more shots were fired, two into the prostrate man and one that went wild, causing the patrons to run for the exits. From my chair I watched as blood from Hardin's wounds and his brains seeped out upon the floor.

"The tension was broken when the swinging doors opened with a bang and young Selman entered hurriedly. He took Old John's smoking gun, saying, 'Don't shoot him anymore—he's already dead.' For a brief moment he scrutinized me and the two cattlemen, then led the limping constable out of the saloon.

"'By Gad!' one of the cattlemen exclaimed. 'I knew it was coming but I thought it would turn out different. I would have bet on Wes Hardin killing John Selman.'

"The other said: 'Old John sneaked in and shot Wes when he wasn't looking.'

"A crowd began to gather, but no one was permitted to enter

the saloon. A man of authority [Justice of the Peace Howe] came in and examined the body. As it was placed on a stretcher, I saw that the back of the head was a gory mass. [Hardin also had been shot in the right side of the chest, and in the right arm.]

"I did not tarry in El Paso. . . an innocent bystander could be easily hurried into the land of no return by bullets from the blazing pistols of those see-red gunmen. I picked up my prisoner and boarded the train that night—Oklahoma bound. It was a grueling trip without sleep, watching my 'bad hombre.' I did not take the handcuffs off him until I had landed him safely in the Guthrie jail.

"Later I heard that Selman claimed self defense. He stated that he had entered the saloon with a man named Shackelford and they had gone to the far end of the bar to drink. While they were drinking, he noticed Hardin watching him closely in the bar mirror. When Hardin thought Selman's eyes were off him, he made a break for a gun in his hip pocket, and Selman immediately pulled his gun and began shooting."

If another man entered the saloon with Selman, McGeeney did not see him; nor did he see that Hardin was armed. "It was deliberate murder. Why did Selman wait so long on the sidewalk for Hardin to come out? And Wes Hardin was not armed."

Selman was tried for the killing, but the jury was unable to reach a verdict. The case was rescheduled for the spring 1896 term of court. About four o'clock the morning of April 5, Selman, in his cups, quarreled with Deputy Marshal Scarborough at the Wigwam Saloon, and was shot to death by Scarborough after they had gone into the alley to "talk over their difficulty." Scarborough won an acquittal, but resigned as deputy marshal and went to work as a detective for a cattlemen's association in New Mexico. On April 5, 1900, near San Simon, Arizona, he was badly wounded while pursuing some members of Butch Cassidy's infamous Hole-in-the-Wall gang, and died at Deming.

Upon returning to Oklahoma from his *viaje* to Juarez and El Paso, McGeeney "found U.S. Marshal Nix in the midst of a fight to oust him from office." While Nix was proud of, and most citizens lauded, his efforts in "weeding out" a great number of notorious desperadoes, many prominent individuals and groups dominating the political scene demanded his scalp because of "extravagant expenses run up against the counties of the Territory"

Patrick Sylvester McGeeney and his wife Mary (nee: Graham) of St. Marys, Kansas (wedding photo).

The McGeeney twins, John Graham "Jack" McGeeney (left) and Thomas Kelly "Tom" McGeeney.

and the alleged "rotten" conduct and doings of sheriffs, deputy sheriffs, and city marshals carrying federal commissions. The paucity of evidence brought to Attorney General Judson Harmon in Washington resulted in a full-scale investigation by Department of Justice inspectors and a grand jury. Although no indictment was brought, Nix was relieved of his duties on January 24, 1896. Following a "merry war" in all political circles—Democratic, Populist, and Republican—Patrick S. Nagle, a young lawyer from Kingfisher, became Oklahoma Territory's new United States marshal.

Nagle reappointed most of the experienced manhunters like Thomas, Tilghman, and Colcord, but reduced the field force from one hundred to thirty-five, with a managing deputy in each judicial district. M.J. Kane of Kingfisher became chief deputy, and John Hale was retained as chief clerk at Guthrie. McGeeney was among the many not recommissioned, and his work as a lawman in Oklahoma ended.

It appears that McGeeney also took leave of the Santa Fe and Wells Fargo, reverting to his earlier aspirations for the stage. During the next two years he trouped with a stock company through Kansas, Indiana, and Ohio. He makes only passing reference to this period—"there were hardships to that life . . . times when I, along with others, wondered where the next meal was coming from"; but there were "small triumphs" which eventually would lead to his "first real bow in the movie world."

At the turn of the century he became supervisor of Negro track repair crews on the Union Pacific out of Junction City and the division end of the railroad at Wamego. During this period, he resided at Junction City and Belvue, where he met, romanced, and married twenty-four-year-old Mary Graham of nearby St. Marys, Kansas, the daughter of John Graham of Ireland. Mary bore him three sons: Patrick, Jr., born in 1900, and John Graham "Jack" and Thomas Kelly McGeeney, twins, born at Belvue in 1902. The latter twin was named for Thomas Kelly, "Mary's sister's husband—a political boss in Kansas, in the diplomatic service."

With these responsibilities, McGeeney looked for a more profitable future. A railroad syndicate land development scheme in western Missouri "failed to pan out." In 1905 he looked south to the new opportunities for American pioneers in Mexico.

•6
"Don Mick's Secret"

Mexico had wonderfully fertile soil and abundant riches. But she faced the disorder of her people and the backwardness that affected poor Latin American countries. For decades she had sought to attract at least a small portion of the Europeans pouring across the Atlantic into the United States and Canada, theorizing that their diligence would improve both the economy and the population.

Most of the land was held in vast *haciendas* and Indian villages. Good, vacant land had to be found. In 1877 the minister of development had requested the governors of each state to list potential areas for colonization by worthy, hard-working foreigners. This proved sluggish and ineffective.

Under the 1880–1884 administration of General Manuel González (an unsophisticated *conquistador* for whom morality began and ended with generosity to friends and the enjoyment of the fruits of victory in battle), *haciendas* were taken and Indian villages, which had held their lands since before the Spanish Conquest but never acquired legal titles, were robbed or expropriated. American railway builders were pledged from six to nine thousand pesos for every kilometer of road constructed, without inquiring into its utility. Real estate corporations were authorized to survey public lands and to keep one third of what they surveyed, the remainder to be sold on easy terms to generals and politicians. By a new mining code, which modified the old Spanish laws declaring all minerals the property of the state, coal and oil rights were vested in owners of the surface. Thus the government was giving away valuable subsoil deposits.

American and European capital began to pour in; the government's revenue increased considerably. But its lavish subsidies to railways and the graft of generals, bureaucrats, and corporations cast their shadow over the treasury. By the end of González' term, the government was on the verge of collapse. Riots, bloodily suppressed, swept Mexico City.

International pleasure was expressed when Porfirio Díaz resumed the presidency and set to work to stave off disaster. A native of the state of Oaxaca, Díaz had received a classical education at the Oaxaco Institute; studied law and military science; and served in the national guard during the war with the United States in 1846–1847. He left the army on Antonio Lopéz de Santa Anna's accession to the dictatorship but returned to play a conspicuous role in the revolution of 1854. He took the field against the French, and was taken prisoner but escaped, and harassed Emperor Maximilian's troops until surrender at Oaxaca. He besieged and captured Puebla in 1867, and immediately marched on Mexico City, which surrendered to him on June 21. On reestablishment of the republic he was an unsuccessful candidate for president. Beginning in 1872 he led revolutions against the government, again occupying the capital in 1876. In 1877 he was elected to fill the unexpired term of the fugitive president, Lerdo de Tejada. Except for the interval when González held the office under the Plan of Tuxtepec (during which Díaz served as chief justice of the supreme court and governor of Oaxaca), Díaz won the presidency repeatedly. The Plan of Tuxtepec, with its promises of effective suffrage and no reelection, was forgotten.

Díaz continued to sell public lands, encourage colonization, and to subsidize communications and transportation. But he bought off political opponents, monopolies and government contracts, cancelled government mortgages, consolidated the internal debt, induced foreign bond holders to accept reduced rates of interest, and otherwise moved Mexico toward its standing as a progressive nation. In 1905 the aging, white-haired general was beginning his seventh term. Díaz, in essence, *was* Mexico.

Most of the colonists in the country had committed themselves to agriculture and were located in northern and southwestern Tamaulipas near the Mexican Central Railway or along the Gulf

Coast. The far western state of Sonora had received a great deal of attention from mining men and investors—cattle raising was the second highest rated industry with wealth estimated in the millions. Chihuahua and Durango, relieved of the Indian scourge of the 1880s, looked to the prospect of extending settlements into the hitherto desolate regions east and north. Schemes for colonizing many other districts were being formed, stimulated by the extension of the railways. Over 100,000 foreigners were now resident in Mexico, and to Mexico's chagrin, nearly a third were Americans. At Ensenada, for example, Americans outnumbered Mexicans 100 to 1, and one Mexican newspaper predicted "annexation by the United States of our frontier territories."

The natives were cautious in sharing their heritage with outsiders. Despite improvements in communications and transportation, most areas remained isolated. Travel from one village to another was over rough trails by burro and mule pack, and settlers feared for their safety against *bandidos* and the arbitrariness of *rurales* or other Mexican officials.

Nonetheless, colonization increased under the Díaz government. The 1902 colonization and naturalization laws of the republic allowed an individual either to claim up to 6,177 acres and purchase it over a ten-year period or to claim 247 acres free, if one-tenth of it were cultivated for five years. Colonists also were exempt from military service and all taxation, except municipal, and they were entitled to bounties for introducing up-to-date machinery and modern methods.

Patrick Sylvester McGeeney was interested in building railroads and moved his family to Mexico City. "During 1906, 1907 and 1908 I was superintendent of construction on the Mexican Central Railway under President A.A. Robinson, when the company decided to extend the road on the Guadalajara Division from Tuxpan, the end of the line, to Colima. . . . My job was to take topography and photographs of the most feasible route through the mountains of the states of Jalisco and Colima, then construct the link between Tuxpan and Colima and standardize the narrow gauge line from Colima to Manzanillo, a port on the Pacific Coast."

He describes this first assignment in an article titled "Don Mick's Secret": "Mounted on Spanish mules, Mr. Voss, my assistant, and I rode out of Tuxpan. The country was sparsely settled, owing to its gigantic roughness—towering mountains, deep barrancas, volcanic rock, huge trees and heavy brush. . . a vast, unconquered wilderness. We spent a month at our arduous task. Then, out of food, we headed our mules toward a little pueblo called Tonilita.

"All day we rode, inspecting the country through binoculars to catch sight of some habitation where we might refresh the inner man. By nightfall we were hopelessly lost. We gave the mules a free rein and allowed them to pick their own course in the darkness.

"We had proceeded in silence for some time when my mule stopped near a small tree and refused to go further.

"I called to Voss: 'We camp here.'

"We removed our saddles, unrolled our blankets, and without inspecting our surroundings, threw our tired, hungry bodies upon the ground and were soon sound asleep.

"I awoke at daybreak and gazed around, dumfounded. We were atop a bald mountain, a scant fifty feet in circumference, with a sheer drop of over a thousand feet on all sides.

" 'Voss!' I yelled. He sat up with a start, saw our predicament and demanded: 'How did we get here?'

"I pointed to a natural bridge about thirty feet long and three feet wide, leading to the mountain top.

" 'Those crazy mules!' Voss exclaimed.

"I trained my binoculars on the mesas below, and saw something move, slowly—a man with rifle in hand, following a game trail.

" 'Wait here, Voss, while I interview the gentleman.' "

McGeeney crossed the bridge cautiously. He saw nothing more of the hunter until he looked over the rimrock—and into the bore of his rifle. "He was an old man in patched clothing. . . neither *mestizo* nor Indian. . . with long hair and a heavy beard that almost covered his features. He inspected me from head to foot.

" 'My partner and I are locating the route for a new railway,' I explained. 'We are lost and hungry.'

"A shadow of understanding crossed his face. He lowered his rifle and spoke in Spanish:

" 'Come with me.'

"I signaled Voss to saddle the mules and follow. Down the mountain, through heavy growth, he guided us to a cave. There, in faultless English, he addressed us:

" 'Gentlemen, my home is at your orders. Please be seated.'

"He entered the cave, and we could hear him conversing with someone in Spanish. . . . Our breakfast consisted of tortillas, frijoles and *agua del coco* . . . . Then the old man came from the cave leading by the hand a girl almost grown to womanhood, dressed in rags, her bare feet in sandals.

" 'Gentlemen, my daughter, Carmen!'

"She came near us, a sad smile hovering around her expressive mouth. In a soft, soothing voice she said: 'Gentlemen, I am pleased to meet you.' Then, as if in shame, she hung her head.

"Voss and I exchanged glances. Such a beautiful face, such refinement, such rags. What mystery surrounded these two?

"We conversed on the topics of the day. The girl was deeply interested in what was happening in the outside world.

" 'Perhaps these gentlemen can help us, *padre mi.*'

" '*Mi dulce corazon,* do not burden them with our sorrow.'

"Voss and I offered to assist them in any way possible.

"The old man said: 'I am an outlaw—'

" 'No, no, *padre mi!*' the girl interrupted. 'Let me tell our story.'

"He remained silent. She became the narrator.

" 'My father incurred the displeasure of the Governor. Our *hacienda* was taken. Father protested. He was placed in jail and sentenced to be shot. Some of our good friends liberated him on the eve of his execution. After much suffering and narrow escapes, disguised in these old clothes, we reached this cave. We were without money. Our food had been exhausted. But we never neglected to pray. We could go no further. Here we fell asleep to await the end.

" 'How long we slept we do not know. When I staggered weakly to the entrance of the cave and into the sunlight, I tripped over a *mecate* bag. Curiosity impelled me to open it. Food! Food in abundance greeted my eyes.

" ' "Come, *padre mi!*" I called. "Our prayers have been answered!"

" 'When father looked into the bag, he dropped to his knees and chanted the Te Deum!

" 'As the days passed, the unseen hands placed food at the entrance of the cave. With the game father kills we have not been hungry. But I long for some clothes, for the companionship of refined people.'

"Tears came into her eyes, and a sob escaped her lips.

" 'There, there, *mi dulce corazon!*' Her father caressed her. 'Be brave! Out of bondage God will deliver us.' "

Struck by the girl's beauty, McGeeney asked to photograph her. " 'Photograph?' she repeated. 'Oh, I have nothing to wear.' Again sadness came into her eyes. '*Padre mi,* may I pose for the gentleman?'

" '*Mi chica de los ojos brillantes,* if it will give you any happiness, yes.'

" 'Excuse me, gentlemen!' Into the cave she went and returned carrying two beautiful shawls of Old Spain. 'While in Paris I saw "The Divine Sarah" [Sarah Bernhardt]. She so impressed me that I have always wanted to be an actress. May I pose as I wish?'

"My camera was ready. With deft fingers she fastened one shawl over the entrance of the cave, and knelt before it, draped in the other.

" 'Now I am an Indian princess praying to a god.'

" 'What next?' I asked, as I snapped her.

"Arising, she placed an *olla* on her shoulder and said: 'An humble *aguadora!*'

" 'Will you give me the pictures?' she asked.

" 'As many copies as you wish, on my return.'

"Early next morning Voss and I bade the two good bye."

Another month elapsed before McGeeney and his assistant completed their survey and returned to the cave. Carmen and her father had vanished. After camping there a night and a day without seeing any sign of them, the Americans rode on to Tonilita.

On the town's dusty street they passed a man whom they mistook for an old peon. McGeeney showed him the photographs and, in Spanish, asked if he had seen the girl and her father. "He looked up from under his shabby sombrero and laughed.

" 'What the divil ails ye? Can't ye speak yer own language? Ye dirty blackguards, did ye find the route for yer railroad?'

"We were surprised by his Irish brogue and that he knew our business.

" 'Come,' he said, in a kindly voice. 'Put up yer mules. We'll have a wee drop and a gabfest.'

"In a cantina we ordered drinks. The old Irishman proved a

rara avis.

"'I'm known as "Don Mick," *jefe* of Tunilita—a Johnny Reb. Came in with General Joe Shelby, and here to stay. . . . Interested in the pretty colleen, are ye? I trust ye to keep my secret of the cave dwellers.'

"He studied me with his keen blue eyes, then continued:

"'I have a rich working mine, but in me blood I've got that look-into-the-ground fever and still roam the mountains and barrancas searching for pay dirt. One day, unknown to him, I followed the old man to the cave, and I saw the colleen. I recognized them as General Alvarez and his daughter. He is a Spanish nobleman. She was educated in Madrid and Los Angeles. And they were living in that cave without comforts of any sort. That night I placed a sack of food near the entrance. . . kept them supplied. . . they did not know where it came from.

"'Two days after your departure, some *rurales* came looking for them. I told the *rurales* I had seen a man and woman riding over the Knife Back for Tuxpan, and they rode away. That night I saddled two gentle mules, tied a small pack of food behind one of the saddles. . . guided the General and his daughter to the *casa* of a friend in Colima and furnished them clothing.

"'What a change the new dress made in the wee colleen! She acted like a bird released from a cage. . . .'

"Don Mick paused in his narrative to light his pipe.

"'Four days we remained in hiding. Any gossip we heard came from the lips of our host. Finally the General told his daughter:

"'"*Mi dulce corazon,* the time has come. I have some business to transact. Do not leave the *casa.*"

"'"Be careful, *padre mi!*" she begged. . . .

"'"Get the mules, Don Mick," the General said. "A little ride will do us both good."

"'Out of the pueblo we rode. "Where to?" I asked.

"'"An interview with the Governor."

"'It was almost midnight when we reached the *hacienda.* Near the *zaguan* we dismounted. "Stay here," ordered the General. "Give me your machete."

"'The darkness swallowed him. In fifteen minutes he returned, minus the machete. Out of hearing of the *hacienda* we put spurs to our mules. Before daybreak, we were in our beds. . . .

"'I joined the General and his daughter at breakfast. Shouts and confusion sounded outside. Our host entered the dining room.

" ' "*Senores,* the Governor was assassinated last night. Someone chopped him to pieces!"

" ' "Too bad, too bad," said the General, as he drained the last drop of chocolate from his cup. Earnestly he gazed into my eyes. He knew that I understood.

" 'When the excitement had abated, we boarded the train for Manzanillo. We arrived in time for the General and his daughter to take passage on a tramp steamer, coastward bound. I placed a small fortune in his hand and watched till the ship was out of sight.'

"With a twinkle in his eye, Don Mick dropped back into his Irish brogue:

" 'Ye spalpeens, ye'll be keeping my secret, won't ye?' "

McGeeney concludes, "Satisfied in my mind that Don Mick is now prospecting over the Great Divide, I am giving his secret to the world. *Requiescat in pace!*"

Patrick Sylvester McGeeney as superintendent of construction on the Mexican Central Railway, Colima-Manzanillo extension (c. 1906).

•7
"Siete Pistolas"

After a route for the railroad had been approved by the Central Railway officials and contractors were hard at work grading, blasting, and drifting tunnels, McGeeney began laying track at Tuxpan. "The necessary material was shipped by boat to Manzanillo and there loaded on the narrow gauge to Colima. A standard gauge locomotive was taken apart, loaded on narrow gauge flat cars and also taken to Colima. When the locomotive was reassembled and ready for the road, I hired an oldtime roadmaster named Richardson, two conductors and two engineers, and put Richardson in charge with authority to hire and fire any man who got drunk or did not hit the ball. As the construction of this gap had to be completed on scheduled time, I instructed my warfinger at Manzanillo to standardize the track, when he was not busy unloading ships. . . .

"Satisfied with the plans I had made, I returned to Mexico City to give my attention to other construction that was being done in several divisions."

The work did not progress as smoothly as expected, however. McGeeney explains in his opus titled "Siete Pistolas" [Seven Pistols]. "I felt an adverse wave that meant trouble. . . knew it for a certainty when Richardson burst into my office two days later.

"He was a sight to behold—unshaven, dirty, his clothes in tatters. He looked like he had been through a sausage mill.

"'Sit down,' I said, kindly. 'What are you doing away

from Colima?'

"His eyes flashed fire from under shaggy brows.

" 'Them damned savage Yaquis you hired didn't know anything about track work. When I tried to show them what to do, they tried to take my scalp. I barely escaped.'

" 'Are you going back to Colima?'

" 'Hell, no! No more Yaquis for me!'

"I gave him his time check, and that was the last I saw of old Richardson."

McGeeney had a waiting list. From it he picked a big Mexican track foreman named Chavez. He looked part Yaqui, so McGeeney thought he would be able to handle the Indians at Colima.

"When I told him of Richardson's trouble, he threw out his chest, thumped his wishbone, and said:

" 'I'm not afraid of them! I'll tame the whole tribe.'

" 'Chavez, I'm sending you to Colima to build a railroad, not to start a war. I want the track laid as quickly as possible.'

"Within three weeks, unannounced, he came into my office. Surprised, I asked:

" 'Now what has happened to you?'

" 'Oh, Senor, me sick—me got *calentura. Muy malo* climate.'

" 'Chavez, you look robust enough to me. I'll diagnose your problem—you haven't got *calentura,* you've got a bad case of Yaqui fever.'

"He hung his head in reply. He told me the conductors and engineers at Colima were drunks. I sent him back to his job.

"Perplexed and undecided, I called on my boss, Mr. Kingman, the Chief Engineer. 'What's on your chest, young man?' He stared at me over his glasses. 'Spit it out!'

" 'Mr. Kingman, the Yaquis tried to scalp Richardson and have inoculated Chavez with *calentura.* If we expect to complete the Colima-Manzanillo extension on time, I guess I'll have to handle the work myself.'

" 'Who will take care of your office here?' he asked.

" 'If it's agreeable, Mr. Kingman, I'll pass the buck to you until I return.'

"He was thoughtful for a moment. 'Those Yaquis are bad hombres. If big Chavez could not handle them, what do you propose to do?'

" 'I won't know until I'm on the ground... but I'm going to construct that line or die in the attempt.'

"Mr. Kingman's eyes twinkled. 'If you can handle the Yaquis as well as you did those track laying blacks on the Union Pacific [in Kansas], the line should be completed on schedule. Go to it, young man.' "

Accompanied by two conductors, two engineers, and office assistant Frank Gordon (his "man Friday"), McGeeney took the first train to Guadalajara. After four days of long, hard riding muleback over the mountains, they reached Colima, a "neat little city" of about 25,000. "I discharged the drunks and checked on the number of laborers. They consisted of one Yaqui chief, Sorio, and forty-six of his *amigos.* The track had been laid only eight kilometers to Las Canas. The Missouri Valley Bridge Company was completing a bridge over the barranca.

"My man Friday was brown skinned and blue eyed. I didn't know what breed he belonged to, and didn't care—he had always been steady and reliable. He spoke no pure *castellano,* but Mexican, and knew how to handle Mexicans. I didn't know how he would stack up with the Indians. I sent him to the highways and byways to recruit men. I could have used six hundred to a thousand. In a few days we had an even hundred, mostly Yaquis.

"The Yaqui chief was suspicious of me and went around armed with a pearl-handled, nickel-plated .32 revolver... watched me more than he did the men over whom I placed him as foreman. I knew that behind his eyebrows he was plotting to get rid of me. So I began to plan to put him on the defensive.

"Luck played into my hands."

Late in the afternoon, McGeeney was in his narrow gauge car on the sidetrack at Coquimatlán finishing his work schedule for the following day, when the train pulled in to take his car to Colima. "As the train stopped, six *rurales* rode up and their Cabo asked where he could find the *jefe* of construction. Pancho, my cook, told him I was in the car. Then my man Friday came up alongside and spoke to me through the open window:

" 'The Cabo is a bad hombre called Siete Pistolas.'

"I told Friday to invite him into the car and bring the Yaqui chief, Sorio, with him. When they had entered and were seated, I said: 'Frank, ask the Cabo why he came to see me....'

" 'Well, Captain, he would like to know when you are going

to pay your men, as he must collect taxes on them.'

"'Taxes did you say, Frank?'

"'One peso per man, Captain—but take it from me, it's a holdup.'

"'All right, Frank. Come here while I write your instructions.'

"He stepped to my desk, and I scribbled on a piece of paper: 'When I say "Seguro Miguel," you cover Sorio with your gun. I'll handle the Cabo.'

"Friday read the note and put it in his vest pocket. 'I'll attend to it at once, Captain.'

"'Tell the Cabo I'll pay him now, but I want a receipt for my money.'

"The Cabo agreed to my demand, with a smile. He wrote a receipt, which I folded and laid on my desk.

"'Senor Jefe,' he asked—his smile vanished—'where is the *dinero?*'

"'Pardon my thoughtlessness!' I opened my desk drawer where I kept my .45 Colt. As my fingers closed around the butt of the weapon, I shouted: 'Seguro Miguel, here's your *dinero!*'

"I poked the Cabo in the nape of the neck with my Colt and he wilted in his chair. Friday's pistol had covered the Yaqui chief, who sat blinking his eyes like an owl in the sunlight.

"'Pancho!' I called.

"'*Aqui,* Senor!' Pancho hurried into the car.

"'Frisk the Cabo and the Chief. I want them disarmed.'

"The Cabo was plentifully supplied with play toys...one big toad sticker and seven loaded pistols of different breeds and nationalities. Sorio traveled light, his only weapon being his .32 revolver.

"'I will keel you, Jefe!' the Cabo snarled.

"'Frank, tell him to shut up or I'll kill him here and now.' Again I jabbed my Colt into his neck. He winced and remained quiet.

"'Pancho, tie the Cabo to his chair. I'm going to take him bye bye.'

"The Cabo could see his men through the open window. I kept behind his chair, so they could not see me.

"'Frank, tell the Cabo to order his men to the *carcel* and to take his horse with them; that he is going to Colima to collect some overdue taxes.'

"The Cabo complied, meekly, and the *rurales* rode away.

"Conductor Willoughby, in charge of the train, came into the car. 'All set,' I said. 'Let's hit the cinders.'"

An hour later the train rolled into Colima. Each evening McGeeney's good friend, Salvador Ochoa, would send his carriage to the station to take McGeeney to the Hotel California, where he was stopping. "On this evening, I instructed the driver to take us to the Governor's office. By chance we found Governor Enrique de la Madrid at his desk. While Friday stood guard over our prisoners, I made my complaint.

"Governor de la Madrid did not relish my treatment of Siete Pistolas, but I made him understand in a very few words that if he did not control his *rurales,* I would take the matter up with President Díaz. It was a known fact that Siete Pistolas collected taxes, as he called them, every payday at the construction camps. The contractors feared him, and I meant to break up his nice little racket.

"The Governor promised that Siete Pistolas would collect no more taxes; that if he continued to do so, he would be sent to hibernate for a time in Belem [the national prison]."

On the way to the hotel, McGeeney explained to Chief Sorio that he was protecting him and all his men against the likes of Siete Pistolas; that he was the Jefe and would treat everybody right, but if they should tread on his coattails, he would "start the celebration" with hot lead and powder smoke. "The next day I noticed a great change in my Indians. They were puzzled, Friday told me, and it was becoming a common saying that I was a brave man to take in the *malo* Pistolas and present him to the Governor. They watched me in awe when the train arrived at the end of the track.

"I told Friday I wanted Chief Sorio and four of his men with a push car loaded with shims, boat spikes, track jacks, levels and spike mauls; that I was going to take them with me and teach them to shim up bridges and level those out of line that had been cribbed up.

"'But, Captain,' he protested, 'Sorio will kill you.'

"'The Chief is all right, Frank,' I said. 'Someone has been mistreating him and his men, and they resent it. Bring Sorio to me when you have the push car loaded.'

"Shortly, Friday and the Chief came into my car. Sorio was carrying his artillery, as usual.

"'Pancho!' I called.

"'*Aquí,* Senor!' he replied, coming from his small kitchen.

"I unbuckled my belt and handed him my holster and .45 Colt. 'Take care of them for me,' I said.

"Sorio watched intently, but I pretended not to notice him. Then he said to Friday, in Spanish: 'Ask the Jefe to excuse me for a few minutes.'

"I granted the request, and he left the car, to return minus his revolver.

"Again I pretended not to notice. I seated myself on the front of the push car and he shook his head as the car gained momentum down a two per cent grade."

Sorio proved an apt pupil. He learned to shim up the first bridge, and seemed proud of his work. "When we reached the second bridge, I told him I wanted two of his men to take me back to the train in the push car; that I would send the car back to him, and when he finished shimming up the bridges to report to me.

"'Sí, Senor Jefe. *Yo se componer puentes.*'

"Later in the afternoon he returned and told me the *puentes* were all *bueno* [bridges were good].

"Friday was with him. 'Frank, advise all the foremen that I will begin the task work tomorrow. I shall pay them time and a half every Sunday they may work. There will be no more cursing and fighting on the job.'

"Friday explained my new rules to the men while the engine was being coupled to the train that would take them back to night camp. As they climbed aboard the flat cars, they began shouting: 'Viva! Viva! Viva el Jefe!'"

There were no more "black looks" from the Yaquis. Construction proceeded "like clockwork."

McGeeney's handling of Siete Pistolas also "enhanced his popularity with the good people of Colima," who knew the *rurale* chief to be a dangerous man. "Every afternoon men and women came down to meet the train and shake my hand for making it possible for them to go to Mexico City and elsewhere via the new railway. When they went on picnics, I allowed them the use of the train without charge, taking them out in the morning and returning them in the evening.

"I was invited into the homes of prominent people, such as

Senora Santa Cruz, the widow of an ex-Governor. She called me a "real caballero" after I told her of my *esposa* and three small sons in Mexico city. That made a hit with the men. They knew I wouldn't flirt with their wives and daughters."

Construction of the Colima-Manzanillo extension was completed by 1908, and McGeeney was placed in charge of three roadmasters and their gangs "doing important repairs" on the Cuernavaca division south of Mexico City. This work was completed "sooner than expected" in light of the number of men the company was able to employ. "The only country where we could obtain laborers was Japan. The Russian-Japanese war was over and thousands of Japanese were brought over to work for our contractors during 1906, 1907 and 1908. They soon disappeared, however, and I am safe in saying they drifted into California, or [were lost] in the many holes in the waters of the Pacific.

"In the meantime, President Robinson of the Mexican Central resigned and Samuel Wilson of the C. & A. was appointed to succeed him. As we could not speak C. & A., he brought some of his pets with him and put the boots to me and others. I became a conductor on the National Lines between San Luis Potosí and Gonzales Junction [with runs through San Miguel de Allende and Acambara to Cuernavaca]."

•8
Stien's Pass and *Cross Timbers*

At Potosí one evening, McGeeney was introduced to an American news correspondent, in Mexico to investigate the marijuana evil. "The man had spent some time trying to get first hand information on the habit and was told I could help him. . . . I had first come upon *mareguana* while superintendent of construction on the Central Railway in 1906. Hundreds of Mexicans working under me were addicts. When they used the stuff, it required several other workers with pick handles and other weapons to subdue them. . . . I explained that the fuzzy leaf of the weed was plucked and dried, then crumbled and smoked in corn husk cigarettes, and packed anything from euphoria to a knockout punch.

"The correspondent did not believe me and decided to try it himself. A few cigarettes made him insane. He broke all the furniture in his hotel room and piled it in the middle of the floor. The hotel management had to send six or seven men to overpower him, so unearthly was the frenzied smoker's strength. They placed him in a padded cell for fifteen days, during which time his mind was a blank. When he recovered, he had no idea of where he had been or what he had done."

A few weeks later, McGeeney "narrowly escaped death" due to the weed. "It was by a queer twist of fate. A Mexican brakeman had been assigned to me for duty. I sent him to serve on another train. He proved to be a *mareguana* addict, and in a frenzy disemboweled his conductor."

McGeeney had some pleasant memories of Cuernavaca. "There I met all classes of people, among them a high born Spanish gentleman, Major Anton Barranache. An officer in Maximilian's ill-fated army too old for regular service, he was appointed custodian of Broda Gardens, the summer home where the unfortunate Empress Carlota spent a few happy hours in 1866 when her husband was emperor of Mexico. His death by a firing squad at Querétaro in 1867 remains a dark page in the history of that country. How this beautiful woman must have suffered. She passed to her reward, always calling the man she loved 'My Maximilian.' I was greatly impressed by the many stories about this royal couple which came from the lips of Major Anton.

"The old gentleman remained faithful to his trust. After the castle fell into decay, he guarded it, ever watchful and waiting for the return of the empress.

"One day the portal of the *zaguan* fell. It was a shock to Major Anton. With tears in his eyes, a sob in his throat, he said:

"'My good friend, I am sad, no more can I lock the door. I need not the key. If you will accept, I will give you the key as a token of my gratitude for the sunshine you have brought in my lonely years. Take it. . . I shall guard the *zaguan*.'

"With reverence, I accepted the quaint old key. A short time afterward, Major Anton died of a broken heart."

Though a conductor's pay was not as remunerative as that of construction superintendent, McGeeney welcomed the break from feverish and hazardous railway building. His vast larder of experience and firsthand knowledge of frontier characters had become his night-muse, with dime novels and stale newspapers as accompaniment. He put his eldest son Patrick to studying French and Spanish in Mexico City, and found time to seriously pursue the pleasures of the pen. He aspired for the prestige not of a historian but of a realist—to supplement his income by writing swift action in a highly colored style, as he lived, with dialogue that rang true.

His first book-length efforts were *Loraine,* a historical romance of the Old South; *The Viper,* a story of New Orleans; *Helen Knox of Nashville,* a romance of the Spanish-American War; and *The 4-D Ranch,* a story of ranch life in Indian Territory. None of these appealed sufficiently to eastern editors and were relegated to the "family trunk." However, he "made it in Boston," when

Down at Stien's Pass and *Down at Cross Timbers*—two novels written by McGeeney in Mexico, published by the Angel Guardian Press of Boston (1909).

the Angel Guardian Press published two of his novels, *Down at Stien's Pass* and *Down at Cross Timbers,* in the winter of 1909.

Down at Stien's Pass (in the words of the press release) was "the story of a trust placed upon the shoulders of a young engineer, Alden Raymond, and how he carried his burden, without shirking from duty, for long, weary years, and his reward. Interwoven is a beautiful romance. . . introducing such characters as Geronimo, the Apache chief; Billy the Kid, the notorious outlaw, and his exterminator, the famous Pat Garrett. . . who, together with the hero, play conspicuous parts in this border drama of New Mexico."

Down at Cross Timbers was described as "a Romance of Old Missouri. . . touching the lives of some simple but beautiful people who inhabit the lonely north range of the Ozarks. . . . The unique version of Bill Childers' first visit to St. Louis during the Carnival of the 'Veiled Prophet' is interesting throughout. . . . Jack Laudon shows a grim determination to succeed—and he does—although confronted by numerous and seemingly insurmountable barriers which block his rugged trail of love. . . . The author knows personally of what he writes. . . . In one instance, he declares that the natives never wear shoes and when a traveler passing through the mountains alighted with but one shod foot, they gathered around the footprint and offered a passerby a reward if he would tell them the name of the 'strange animal.'"

Both novels bore frontispiece portraits of McGeeney's twin boys and were affectionately dedicated "to Jack and Tom." They were priced at two dollars each and distributed in Mexico by the American Book and Printing Company.

Stien's Pass "is a beautiful story without a peer," said the New York *World. Cross Timbers* "is true to life. . . Opie Reid has met his master," opined the San Francisco *Call,* and the Kansas City *Journal* commented: "We have read with pleasure and consider the book a masterpiece."

The *Mexican Herald* (Mexico City) observed: "*Down at Stien's Pass* is a beautifully told romance which embodies much of the Western chivalry the American has learned to love." And of *Cross Timbers:* "There is no lack of local color. . . . The author pictures his characters as they were or are, as is proven by the intimacy with which he speaks. Mr. McGeeney is one of the new railroad school that has already produced some good story tellers, Bliss

Carmen and Jack London, for example. Their training was not so much of the arts and muses, but they ventured and learned to know the people of whom they wrote. . . . Today Mr. McGeeney is a conductor on the National Railways of Mexico, and so much for that, for he is now studying what will probably prove the foundation for his next effort."

The following January, McGeeney vacationed with his family in Kansas, stopping en route at San Antonio, Texas, where his books were "on sale at Aguas" and reviewers were impressed. Wrote the San Antonio *Express,* "The volumes are well written, the color of the West is faithfully reproduced, and the narratives never lose their interest or sparkle." The San Antonio *Gazette* agreed, "They are worth reading."

At Newton, the *Evening Journal* proclaimed, "All Newton has reason to congratulate itself that it has numbered among its former residents a real live and successful author in the person of P.S. McGeeney, who grew to manhood here, and is still in close touch with the town and its people through his mother and sister [Elizabeth Chapman]. There is no doubt that those who remember the author, as well as all who take pride in the advancement of a Newton man, will avail themselves of the privilege of reading *Down at Stien's Pass* and *Down at Cross Timbers,* which can be obtained at Phil Anderson's."

While in Newton, McGeeney "addressed council No. 786, Knights of Columbus. . . of which he has long been a brother. . . at a meeting of those members in the Knights of Columbus Hall." He told his listeners of his recent experiences at San Luis Potosí and Cuernavaca, and to the *Journal* office he "entrusted" the key to the portal of Broda Gardens, "making a beginning toward a city museum, when it will be placed among the relics."

This prompted a call from the editor of *The Kansas Magazine,* established in 1872 and now a bright literary memory. The editor requested "some articles, illustrated, from Old Mexico. . . of which you have learned so much." McGeeney suggested a piece on "What Kansans Have Done for Mexico," and the editor agreed: "It is rich in possibilities. . . . Your friends will doubtless look forward to this future effort."

Among the bits of Kansas news appeared an obscure item stating that Mexican families at Wellington were growing marijuana for a narcotic drink. Wellington authorities had communicated with state officials and found there was no Kansas law against growing or using the plant. McGeeney was "immediately attracted to its importance" while promoting his books in Wichita, and declared to the editor of the *Eagle,* "The weed is unusually strong and demoralizing in its effects. It makes men absolutely crazy, wild and uncontrollable. Texas is fighting the stuff. . . . The mayor of San Antonio has forbidden growing of *mareguana* in that city, and I believe the mayor of Wellington might well take the same step. State lawmakers should speedily quash any attempt to introduce it into Kansas. It would be a terrible thing should use of the weed become a habit or common among our young people. . . ." McGeeney was ahead of his time.

On return with his family to Mexico, he had a "second look" at San Antonio. It was a colorful, historic city with beautiful parks and gardens, situated astride the San Antonio River, which was fed by a cluster of deep springs to the north and flowed steadily southeast, spanned by numerous bridges and aqueducts in the business and residential districts. Its mild climate attracted visitors the year around. It featured band concerts, fiesta parades, the old Spanish town from which it developed, called "La Villita," and imposing adobe structures nearly 200 years old: Mission San Francisco de la Espada; Mission Nuestra Senora de la Purisima Concepción de Acuna; queen of the missions, San José y San Miguel de Aquayo; and most importantly, the Alamo, "Cradle of Texas Liberty," where during thirteen days in 1836 a little band of 185 Texas patriots were slain in battle against the overwhelming Mexican forces under Santa Anna.

The first Irish settlers in Texas built colonies near Refugio, Victoria, and Goliad, but had been forced to move to San Antonio for protection from tribes of Indian marauders and because their crops had been destroyed during the Revolution. Their houses of adobe, logs, and other materials built along North Alamo, Avenue E, and Nacogdoches Street resembled their homes in the old country. This section of the city was called "Irish Flats." A number of early German settlers, who arrived at Matagorda Bay on the Gulf to carve a place for themselves in the Texas wilderness and found their way to San Antonio, lived in La Villita. Many occupied the old Spanish houses, modified with steeper roofs like those in the mother country, or had built new German houses. Alsatians, Swiss, Belgians, and Dutch further enriched the city's heritage. Although more than a score of racial groups were represented, its populace was predominantly American and Spanish.

During the 1870s and 1880s, the city thrived on the trade of immigrants and cattlemen. Saloons and gambling halls flourished. Street cars came before 1890. By 1900 five railroads had built into San Antonio, and it became a wholesale and retail center of 54,000. Industries included flour mills, railroad shops, foundries, and breweries. It also was a military center, with Fort Sam Houston, the nation's largest such establishment and headquarters of the U.S. Army's Southern Department. There were some twenty private schools and colleges, among them St. Mary's University, founded in 1852; the German-English School of Julius Berends, in 1858; San Antonio Female College, in 1894; Our Lady of the Lake, in 1896; and the San Antonio Academy, a preparatory school for boys.

San Antonio remained typically "gay nineties." Automobiles were in vogue, and gasoline was obtained at the drugstore. But there was no traffic problem. The only complaint was with buggy teams and saddle horses that stamped holes in the new pavement on the Alamo and Main plazas.

The city "fascinated" McGeeney. "There is no place on the continent with a more desirable winter climate, not even Mexico," he stated in an interview with the San Antonio *Light*. "I like the city so much, I'm thinking of purchasing property and residing here permanently." He noted San Antonio's "excellent school facilities," adding that young Patrick, Jr., was "receiving a good schooling in French and Spanish, but not English," and wanted his sons educated there.

Back in Mexico, McGeeney headquartered at San Luis Potosí, the terminal for his runs on the National Lines. He never got around to the *Kansas Magazine* article. By midsummer, *Stien's Pass* and *Cross Timbers* were in their fifth printing. There was even more interesting news from the Guardian Angel Press—the books were under consideration by the great dramatist, actor, and producer, David Belasco.

During his lifetime (1854–1931), Belasco wrote and adapted seventy-five plays and made pioneer contributions to realistic staging. Born in San Francisco, he began his acting at age eleven. As a teenager he toured with stock companies through the small towns and mining camps of California. Coming to New York in 1880, he became a stage manager of the Madison Square Theater fame, an exponent of the stock company. An independent producer in 1907, Belasco built his own Broadway theater, the Stuyvesant, later named The Belasco. His current successful plays included *Madam Butterfly* (1900), *The Darling of the Gods* (1902), and *The Girl of the Golden West* (1905).

"There is a fascination surrounding tales of border life that reaches all classes," the Boston publisher wrote McGeeney. "It is of such stories as yours that the modern melodrama is made, and Belasco is likely to immortalize one or both of these stories by placing them on the stage in all the setting and finish that have made Belasco melodrama the wonder of the theatrical world."

The *Mexican Herald* lauded the announcement: "Owing to their large sales and continual demand, *Down at Stien's Pass* and *Down at Cross Timbers*. . . if faithfully copied, properly staged, should draw full houses. . . . Mr. P.S. McGeeney, our well-known railroad man, seems to have a very bright future and his many friends in the republic wish him every success."

Apparently Belasco did not share the enthusiasm. He produced instead *The Return of Peter Grimm* (1911), and McGeeney's "bright future" vanished in the winds of revolution sweeping Mexico.

·9
"Three Days in the Brush"

How Porfirio Díaz was accused of selling out Mexico to foreign companies that worked the peons for slave labor and took the wealth out of the country is a matter of history. Díaz resigned in May of 1911 and fled to France, where he died in 1915. In October of 1911, Francisco I. Madero, the democratic reformer who headed the revolt, became president.

It was a glorious success to those who had starved and smoldered under thirty-four years of Díaz dictatorship and abased themselves before the *jefes políticos,* wont to dispose of malcontents. But from that time until the "Tragic Ten Days" of battle that ended in Madero's assassination on the road near San Luis Potosí and the seizure of power by the mask-faced old Indian killer and reactionary, General Victorio Huerta, almost every man with a gun and a grievance became a guerilla leader, and *federale* generals changed their allegiances so frequently it was impossible to determine who was in charge of anything.

Small groups of unscrupulous murderers and robbers took advantage of the badly disorganized government and began looting and killing ranch people, particularly foreigners and members of the wealthy Mexican class. *Rurales* ordered to run down the bandits often did a little looting on their own. Thousands of colonists abandoned their homes, never to return. Revolution ran riot as armies of *insurrectos,* large and small, descended like a plague and took garrisons, towns, and railroad junctions.

Not a few battles between the revolutionaries and federal forces were fought on the National Lines. One such clash involving McGeeney is described in a segment of his reminiscences titled "Three Days in the Brush." "Frequently, on my layover day at the Potosí terminal, I was called to make a 'San Felipe turn' [leaving in the morning and returning in the afternoon].

"Everything on this day was going in its usual routine. We reached Chirimoya, where our engine took water and the rear brakeman coupled the helper engine, in charge of Engineer Berry, to the rear of the caboose to push us to the top of the high mesa on our last lap to San Felipe. All set, we chugged, chugged to the top. The brakeman pulled the lever, uncoupled the helper engine, and Engineer Berry drifted back down the side of the barranca to Chirimoya.

"As the train stopped on the San Felipe siding, I dropped from the caboose and started to the station. At that moment the engineer, fireman, coal passer, head and swing brakemen came hot-footing it down the track toward me.

"Surprised, I asked the engineer: 'What's wrong with you?'

" 'Revolutionists!' He pointed across the mesa behind the station.

"About a kilometer away I could see a cloud of dust and the bobbing figures of a mob.

" 'Get back to the engine,' I ordered. 'Pick up the caboose and we'll high-daddy out of here.'

" 'Not me!' the engineer shouted, as he and the others ran down the track toward Chirimoya.

"My rear brakeman, Pascual Ortiz Rubio, stayed with me.

" 'What are we going to do, *Jefe?*'

" 'Follow me!'

"I registered at the station, gave the waybills to the agent, and reported my arrival to the chief dispatcher at San Luis Potosí. Then Rubio and I hit the ties across the mesa after the rest of the crew."

Not any too soon, however. The revolutionists were already swarming into San Felipe. "Did we run—no, no, not us! We flew. Out of breath, we reached the rimrock of the barranca. There we left the track, found a hiding place in the mesquite brush, and waited.

" 'Are we going to stay here?' asked Rubio, when he had stopped panting.

" 'Just until we've rested—then it's on to Chirimoya.'

"I crawled up and peeped over the rimrock. A great deal of activity was taking place at the station, and as I was watching the scene with interest, something hit the rimrock nearby and screamed 'Pow! Pow! Pow!' at me. Believe me, Jennie Johnson, I needed no further invitation to erase myself from the landscape.

"Rubio sat on the ground as if in a trance. 'Get down!' I warned.

"He paid no attention. Before I could utter another word, a second 'Pow! Pow! Pow!' ordered us to move on. I looked in the direction of the Pow and saw a train carrying some *soldados* had stopped. They were leaving it, deploying around. . . . I started crawling further into the brush, and Rubio crawled after me.

"'Where are we going now, *Jefe?*'

"'To find a better hiding place,' I answered."

Near the bottom of the ravine, they spotted a "small tumbled down *jacal,*" which they reached in safety. "It was all to the mustard, but occupied by a big mamma rattlesnake and her ten healthy children. Papa rattler was absent—probably on a big drunk celebrating the arrival of his little ones. Mamma rattler was *muy bravo* and showed fight. It was necessary for us to execute her and the entire family. . . .

"We had just won our war over the rattlers when the *revoltosos* on the mesa started the ball rolling. Then the *soldados* in the barranca returned the compliment with great vigor. While bullets screamed over the *jacal,* Rubio and I prayed and promised to sin no more. My engineer, fireman, coal passer and brakeman had discovered our 'dobe shelter and crawled in to join us in our resolutions. Every now and then donations of lead would drop in to see if we were in good health and comfortable. The little leaden brothers were so affectionate and solicitous we could smell their breath, which almost caused us to—Well, you may guess the answer to that one."

At sundown the cannonading ceased, and McGeeney realized that he was hungry. "My inner man was bawling out the cook and raising hell with the dining room furniture.

"'Old Top,' I said, to the engineer, 'will you be kind enough to direct me to the nearest restaurant? I'm a stranger here.'

"'Sure, you bloody Yarmouth bloater. The Delmonico is just a short distance from here. You can see it over that large boulder out there.'"

The engineer pointed out a shepherd's hovel on the other

side of the barranca, a quarter-mile away. "'I dined there at the noon hour.'

"'No fooling,' I said.

"'On the square,' he replied with a smile, as he lit his pipe.

"Of course my engineer was a damned liar and an irresponsible hombre. . . .

"A full moon had risen over the mesa [making the night too bright to forage]. I was so damned hungry I could have devoured that mamma snake and finished off the repast with a dessert of the family, if my tonsils hadn't rebelled.

"I settled down in the corner of the little *jacal* and tried to pass off into the land of snores, but I couldn't be impolite to my company—the damned little darling fleas who insisted that I stay awake and entertain them. Did I? You bet, to the best of my ability—scratching. Toward morning, tired out from playing their game, I managed to snatch a little shuteye.

"I was awakened at daybreak by my engineer laying flat on his back in another corner trying to imitate a locomotive whistle at a grade crossing. I was disappointed in him so I sounded my bugle call and my crew sprang into action. . . .

"As the day advanced we dared not leave our hiding place, and when the sun reached its zenith, boy was it hot! Without water, our mouths were full of cotton.

"Relief came as the shades of night again were falling. When it was dark, I dispatched Rubio and Inez [the coal passer] to capture any *comida* they could find. I was thankful when they returned [from a shepherd's hovel] with two large *ollas* of water and plenty of tortillas. Our supper consisted of tortillas and water; breakfast, water and tortillas. Not so good, but better than tackling the dead mamma snake which now sent out an odor positively not of roses.

"Through that long weary third day we hid in the brush with the hot leaden pellets singing 'Nearer My God to Thee!' and the Miserere. Yes, we had a hell of a swell time, and I can sympathize with Napoleon when he was a prisoner on the Island of St. Helena.

"Late in the afternoon we watched the Díaz *soldados* getting ready for a hasty retreat, and in a short time their train backed out of sight around a curve. An hour elapsed before the curtain went up on the next act—our engine and caboose, coupled to a string of box cars filled with the Maderistas, rolled past our hiding place down the grade and out of sight into the barranca.

"We ventured forth and peeped over the rimrock. All was fair and quiet along the Wabash. We hot-footed our brave selves back to the station and reported to the superintendent that, although the enemy had taken our engine and caboose, we had put them to flight. We were ordered to return on the first train to San Luis Potosí.

"We arrived the next morning before daybreak. Our engine and caboose had arrived safely at the terminal. The revolutionists had occupied the city, and as gringos were not popular, it gave me an excuse to stay in my room, there to eat, sleep and doctor the wounds I had received in the endless battle with those cute, affectionate little fleas. God ——— them!"

McGeeney's second brush with the Maderistas came only days later. "Sometimes a fellow has hunches. I had one the morning I left Gonzales Junction, and felt sure something would happen before I piloted my train to San Luis Potosí, the end of my run. My hunch proved true. It happened at San Miguel de Allende.

"As the train stopped at the station, I strode up the platform. No one was in sight. No agent, no operator, no *mozo* to receive the freight I had to unload. Not even the agent's *perro* came to greet me. Up the long sandy street of the little pueblo, nothing stirred. All was as silent as a tomb. I looked through the bay window into the telegraph office. Papers littered the floor. It was evident somebody had ransacked the place.

"I went around the station, calling, '*Oiga! Oiga, agente!*' [Hello! Hello, agent!]

"After repeating the call several times, I heard a muffled answer, 'Senor! Senor! Senor!'

"The voice seemed to come from the ground. I was fully five minutes locating its owner. Behind the depot in the 'what-not,' I found the agent, the operator and the *mozo*. I summoned my three brakemen. With a rope we pulled them out of the cesspool.

" '*Revolutosos!*' the agent exclaimed. 'They left about an hour ago. We hid out!'

" 'Funny place to hide,' I said. 'How many were here?'

" 'About five hundred.'

"In the meantime the frightened *mozo* was high-tailing across the mesa for parts unknown, and the air around the agent and the operator became pungent with a vicious odor.

"'I'll unload your freight at Dolores Hidalgo,' I told the agent. 'You can pick it up tomorrow.' Then suggested: 'You had better go home—that is, if your *esposa* will let you in.'

"With a handkerchief covering my nose, I gave the engineer the highball, and swung into the caboose as it passed. I sent my rear brakeman to tell the engineer to look out for obstructions on the track and not to stop if we sighted the revolutionists.

"About five miles out of San Miguel de Allende, we overtook them. They signaled us to stop and began firing into the air, but we passed them like the Limited passing a tramp.

"'A close call,' I soliloquized. 'A damned close call!'

"For two reasons I shall always remember San Miguel de Allende. One, that pueblo can claim the distinction of having the only Gothic church in Mexico; the other, that terrible odor that came from the clothing of the agent, the operator and the *mozo* after we rescued them from the 'what-not.'"

Railroad conductors and engineers were finding it impossible to make runs without risking their lives. A number of them left the service and returned to the United States to complain to President William Howard Taft. An estimated two billion dollars had been invested in Mexico, more than half of which came from the United States. The Taft administration recognized the Madero regime and embargoed the shipment of munitions to anti-Madero factions; otherwise, it adhered to a policy of nonintervention. When Huerta seized control, the European powers accepted him. President Taft refused recognition despite the pressure from American business interests, the colonists, railroaders, and others. When Woodrow Wilson succeeded Taft as president, he also disapproved of Huerta and announced that the United States would not lend support to special interests.

McGeeney himself found conditions untenable. Too, he feared for the safety of his wife and children. Early in April of 1912, he quit the National Lines and moved his family to San Antonio, then returned to San Luis Potosí to obtain a service letter and reimbursement for travel expenses.

His problems were "entirely unexpected." C.R. Hudson, Vice-Presidente Ejecutive of the railways in Mexico City, rejected his application on April 20: "Mr. E.N. Brown [the new president of the National Lines] has instructions out not to issue transportation" to railway conductors and engineers who "walked off their jobs," and it would be "highly improper for me to do anything contrary to what he has arranged. I am sure, on reflection, you will appreciate my situation fully."

McGeeney's temper flared. He entrained to Mexico City and "discussed the matter with President Brown." Brown expressed "nothing but the most kindly feeling" for the men formerly employed by the National Lines. "They are not only good men, but men [of] whom any railroad system in the world could feel proud," he said. "I had no desire to make reference to or intimate the fact that there was a walk out." But his "hands were tied." As a quasi-official of the Mexican government, he was "bound in his action in the premises to reflect the government's views." No service letters would be issued.

McGeeney's next stop was the American Embassy. Secretary Nelson O'Shaughnessy, a veteran of the American diplomatic service and "a good Irishman," ushered McGeeney into the presence of U.S. Ambassador Henry Lane Wilson. Wilson, already familiar with the matter, praised President Brown: "No one should doubt for an instant that in whatever he has done he has been actuated by the highest motives and by an absolute trust committed to his hands. . . . The American employees were acting within their undoubted rights in leaving an employment which has ceased to offer attractions to them. The situation created was most difficult for Mr. Brown to meet." But the ambassador "had a suggestion."

McGeeney boarded the first train to San Antonio "to confer with railroad men in that city." By month's end, he was back in the Mexican capital as representative of the Order of Railroad Conductors and the Brotherhood of Locomotive Engineers, with an endorsement by their grand officers to his demand for "service letters and transportation for members of the two orders." During a "secret meeting" held upon a special train at the Ruins of Mitla, "between Mexico's president, a member of his cabinet, President Brown and Ambassador Wilson," McGeeney laid his cards on the table. The Order of Railroad Conductors and the Brotherhood of Locomotive Engineers could "call a walk out that would bring virtually every train on the Mexican lines to a standstill."

The results of the meeting were announced by President Brown in the *Mexican Herald* of May 1. "I have assured the representatives of the American railway conductors and engineers who quit their positions on the National Lines that those who paid their fare from Mexico will be reimbursed if they can show a receipt for the money expended. . . .

"Some difficulty presents itself as to the service letter as such letters must state how the men quit their last employment, whether strike, walkout, discharge, or other manner. I have suggested several forms of service letter which would be acceptable to be drawn up by the men and submitted to me for decision, and have added that I would sign such letters as would not be incompatible with my position with the National Lines.

"I believe that the men made a mistake; nevertheless, I am disposed to do anything in my power to help them."

In his verification letter to McGeeney at the Hotel St. Francis, Brown was more placating. "If a service letter which will carry with it some idea of the true conditon [for their departure] is what our ex-foreign employees want, we will consider this and would like to have suggestions from them as to the wording. . . . All of them are at liberty to refer to the officials or myself, and I shall be pleased to answer such references.

"For those employees still here, and who wish to leave Mexico, I will furnish passes to the border if they will call promptly for them."

A letter to McGeeney from Ambassador Wilson on the same date congratulated him "upon the victory you have won in bringing to a happy climax the perplexing and dangerous three-cornered misunderstanding between the Mexican government, the National Railways of Mexico, and the foreign employees. The settling of this matter by you ended international complications . . . and speaks well of your diplomatic ability. . . . I must say that you are the only man who ever made the Mexican government tremble."

McGeeney returned the compliment some time later. "Henry Lane Wilson stayed with me every step of the way. . . . He was a gentleman and a scholar. He had no axes to grind whatever and you could always find him in his office, or make an appointment with him through Secretary Nelson O'Shaughnessy.

"Through sympathy, I spent a great deal of my spare time getting some of our smart, drunken and overbearing gringos out of the *carcels*. I would contact Ambassador Wilson and with his help the matter was placed before President Díaz. After an investigation, nine times out of ten the culprit was freed.

"I cannot speak too highly of Henry Lane Wilson nor list here all the good he accomplished. He was the only real ambassador the American government ever appointed to represent us. . . and all the thanks he received was to be placed upon a pillory of shame because he suggested to our President Woodrow Wilson that he recognize Victoriano Huerta after the assassination of Francisco I. Madero. Huerta was the only man at the time who could have staved off a revolution. I knew the old General; the best people liked him. He was the strong man of Mexico."

McGeeney received his service letter and reimbursement. "Through with foreign railways," he rejoined his family in San Antonio.

·10
The Power of Love

In San Antonio, McGeeney established himself at 2610 North Flores Street, found employment with a local insurance company, and splashed into the Alamo City's cultural life with a new novel, *The Power of Love.* He described his novel as "a double romance, with a grand moral showing the strong, human characteristics of a noble and generous heart. . . returning to life something that has lain dormant and almost forgotten in the mad rush onward in the selfish race to wealth and for POWER."

The theme: "Love does not need to be fostered in a hothouse with the same care as is bestowed upon a delicate flower. Love is engendered into us in our infancy by her who bore us. Love does not need to be awakened, for it never sleeps, and knows when it meets its affinity. Love should be our guiding star in all things that are pure and holy, for without love there can be no happiness."

The action was "set in the Middle West, though later transferred to Kentucky and Tennessee," where "night riding scenes" that were "worked in" evoked from Tennessee's ex-Governor Bob Tayler this afterword, in part: "If I were a sculptor, I would chisel from marble. . . the figure of an Irishman sacrificing his hopes and his life on the altar of his country, and carve on its pedestal the name of [the hero] Robert Emmett. If I were a painter, I would make the canvas eloquent with the deeds of the bravest people who ever lived. . . whose loyalty and devotion to the hopes of free government no tyrant can ever crush. And I would write under the picture, 'Ireland.' If I were a poet, I would weave the shamrock and the rose into garlands of glory for the Emerald Isle. . . the nursery of liberty."

The Broadway Publishing Company of New York, which first saw the manuscript, commented, "It depicts life, East and West, in your usual forceful style. . . what it lacks in erudite specializing is more than compensated for in uniqueness of plot." But the company objected to the story's being "carried from chapter to chapter with prolix filling, which is so often indulged in by many authors to the annoyance of our present day readers." There were rejections by other publishers, including the Angel Guardian Press of Boston.

McGeeney was not discouraged. At first, he considered rewriting the story as a play. According to the San Antonio *Light,* he "spent a day with thirty members of the Orpheus Dramatic Club at the residence of Mr. and Mrs. C.P. Wells on the Concepcion road," where club members "posed before his camera in the beautiful woodlands of the Wells home. . . in typical wild west costumes, which at times were changed for those of night riders to suit the varied situations in the script. . . . In the pictures, the part of the heroine was taken by Miss Courtney Giffen and the two leading male characters by Victor Flato and [D.A.] Weigand."

Then McGeeney had a better idea. He wrote, "To a handful of brave and noble men who have taken on their shoulders a burden, a cross, as it were, of Christian charity, a self-imposed task, so that they may do good unto others without reward, still leaving behind them a monument which explains their conduct of life and of which their progeny shall ever be proud.

"To the members of Bexar County Division No. 1, Ancient Order of Hibernians, I humbly dedicate this work."

The Alamo Printing Company of San Antonio agreed to publish a "Hibernian Edition. . . to be sold for the purpose of raising funds for a National Ancient Order of Hibernian Hospital-Home to be built at Junction City, Kansas."

So that "no doubt might exist as to the excellence" of his work, McGeeney "allowed several people to read the manuscript," and obtained endorsements such as follow:

> I have read *The Power of Love* and am happy to tell you that I find it a good, moral story. . . I have no hesitation in recommend-

ing it. I hope that you may be successful in the charitable enterprise to which I understand you will devote the proceeds.

Wishing you every blessing, I am

Yours faithfully,
J.W. Shaw
Bishop of San Antonio

I have read the Ms. and take pleasure in stating that I found it to be wholesome, entertaining fiction, containing nothing objectionable to faith or good morals. . . .

Very truly yours,
G.A. Fitz Gibbon
San Luis College
San Luis Potosí, Mexico

The Power of Love. What do these words signify? To thoroughly understand them, one must read the story under that title. . . . A strong, beautiful, thrilling love story, treating upon the greatest issue of the day, intense in its magnitude, greater than *The Rosary,* with living, breathing characters that one can close one's eyes and see vividly as they act their parts; such an imagination is beyond description, and coming from the pen of a man of vast experience, who really speaks to you from every line. . . .

Even the most fastidious holy, modest and critical could not take exceptions.

Edmund J. Geehan
City Editor
San Antonio *Express*

With these and other endorsements, McGeeney departed for Kansas. The Junction City *Union* said this of the proposed enterprise: "Plans have been completed in a conference between a committee from the local council of the Knights of Columbus and P.S. McGeeney of San Antonio, Texas, whose latest book, *The Power of Love,* is to be a big factor in raising the bulk of the funds for the hospital. The hospital matter has been under consideration for two years. . . . The work of raising subscriptions is to be started at once. The McGeeney book will be sold for $1.50 per copy, fifty cents of which will go for the hospital building and its maintenance. Each council of the Knights of Columbus will assist in the sale. . . . It is estimated by Mr. McGeeney that one-half of the 350,000 Knights in the United States will purchase books and that the hospital share will reach $87,500. Mr.

McGeeney will have general charge of the sale and will appoint agents in practically every town where there is a Knights of Columbus chapter. The Knights will own the hospital, and a Catholic Sisterhood will be in charge. The building will be erected in or near Junction City.

"Junction City has been selected as a site [because] it is near what has always been known as the geographical center of the United States, and as it is to be the national hospital for the order, it is essential that it be easy of access from all parts of the country. . . . Mr. McGeeney formerly lived in Junction City and has many associations here."

The Newton *Journal* noted that McGeeney "visited with his mother at 1002 Ash Street . . . coming to Newton directly from Junction City. He now returns to San Antonio."

The Power of Love was promoted throughout the United States in 1914, and in Ireland by the Sisters of Charity, Ballagharderreen, County Mayo, and by stationery outlets in Dublin. Hundreds of copies were subscribed to through the efforts of the Bexar County Division No. 1, Ancient Order of Hibernians. Sales, however, "generated only $25,000"—far short of McGeeney's expectations. Nonetheless, the book found wide readership. The Alamo Company reprinted it in 1920.

McGeeney's literary accomplishments also provided an outlet for the talents of Orpheus Dramatic Club members and other San Antonio artists. In 1914 he chaired a special committee on arrangements for the annual St. Patrick's Day celebration, sponsored by the local and state chapters of Hibernians. Nearly every member of the city's Irish community gathered in the Hibernian hall the morning of March 17. At 9:30 they marched in grand procession through the principal streets, headed by a brass band, to St. Patrick's Catholic Church, where the Reverend Father Pinnell officiated at a high mass and delivered the St. Patrick's Day sermon. That evening a crowd of nearly 2,000 jammed the St. Mary's Parochial School hall, where, said the San Antonio *Express,* "an extensive program was given. . . . It was opened with an overture 'Medley of Irish Airs,' by the St. Mary's orchestra, followed by 'An Curet,' sung by the Gaelic class of boys and girls; a violin solo, 'When I Dream of Old Erin,' by Miss Mildred Wiseman; a harp selection by Miss Octavia Bullis; and concluded with the event of the season, a one-act playlet written expressly for the occasion [and directed] by P.S. McGeeney, entitled *'St. Patrick's Night.'"*

The scene was Ireland; the time, the middle of the eighteenth century. The story evolves around the anxiety of Mr. and Mrs. Dan O'Flynn for their son Jimmie, who sailed for America on St. Patrick's night a year previous and has sent no tidings. Their daughter, Mrs. Germie Lafferty, her husband and their two daughters, Tessie and Kitty Lafferty; Terrance O'Neil (a gamekeeper played by McGeeney), in love with Kitty; Jack Horan, in love with Tessie; and Lanty Lannigan, in love with every girl he meets—all attempt to cheer the O'Flynns with their antics and humorous Irish tales. But in vain. Mrs. O'Flynn weeps, and while she is still in tears, Jimmie returns home, bringing with him an American wife. Mrs. O'Flynn rushes into the arms of her son. Dan O'Flynn expounds on how an Irishman, no matter where he roams, is always a true son of Old Erin and never found wanting in celebrating that day of all days so near and dear to every Irish heart. While this happy reunion is taking place, Lanny Lannigan is caught making love to Jimmie's wife. He is advised to join the Mormon church and take a trip to Salt Lake City, Utah. Germie Lafferty appoints himself master of ceremonies and calls upon everyone present to contribute something in honor of Jimmie's homecoming. Behind the scenes, Terrance O'Neil (McGeeney) sings his "Irish Serenade."

In 1915 McGeeney again chaired the St. Patrick's Day celebration, described by the San Antonio *Express* as "the most elaborate in the history of the city. Prominently identified with those in charge of arrangements are the members of the Daughters of Erin, auxiliary to the Ancient Order of Hibernians, organized a few months ago." At nine o'clock the morning of March 17, the Sons of Erin and Daughters of Erin assembled at St. Mary's auditorium. The parade formed on St. Mary's Street, "proceeded up Houston Street, down Commerce to Soledad, thence by way of Houston Street back to St. Mary's. Afterwards, a mass was attended at St. Patrick's Church on Government Hill. . . . The evening entertainment was presented at the Grand Opera House.

"The program opened with an overture, 'Medley of Airs,' by St. Mary's orchestra; 'Let Erin Remember' was sung by the mixed chorus. A dance, 'St. Patrick's Day-in-the-Morning,' was given by the intermediate class of St. Mary's [twelve girls] costumed in white dresses spangled with shamrocks. A vocal solo, 'Dear Little Shamrock,' was sung by P.G. Osborne, and 'An Cruet' was sung by the Gaelic class of boys and girls. A violin solo, 'Old Cabin Song,' played by Master Robert Wallace, was so well encored that he responded with 'Humoresque.' Then came Reverend Father G.P. Mulvaney's lecture. . . .

"Rev. Father Mulvaney's address was a tribute to the Irish people. 'The greatness of a nation,' he said, 'lies not in its material progress alone, but in its morality.' While Ireland was not ranked among the nations of the world as a great power, it was noted for the purity of its women and the great number of saints and martyrs to the church that it had produced. 'The morality of a country depends upon its women,' he continued, 'and the Irish-American women, taken as a class, have done more for the moral uplift of this nation than anything else. . . .'

"His lecture was followed by 'The Harp That Once Through Tara's Halls,' sung by the mixed chorus. Vocal solos, 'Conven Partir,' from *La Figlia,* and 'Kathleen Mavourneen,' were sung by Miss Courtney Giffen. A violin solo, 'Where the River Shannon Flows,' by Miss Mildred Wiseman, received much applause. Miss Josephine Luechese sang 'Micela-Aria' and 'Villa Nella.' A harp solo, 'Oh, Believe Me If All Those Endearing Young Charms,' was given by Miss Octavia Bullis. 'Good-bye' and 'The Last Rose of Summer' was sung by Miss Wilhelmina Russell, a well-known artist of Mexico City, who recently has been studying in Italy."

The program climaxed with "a two-act playlet, *In the Penal Days* [casting fourteen members of the Orpheus Club], written and directed by P.S. McGeeney. . . . This historical drama was laid in Ireland in the Cromwellian period, when the Irish were persecuted by the English [and] involved the fortunes of the Earl of Tyrone, an Irish nobleman, who, because of his fidelity to the Roman Catholic Church, is driven with his beautiful wife from Ireland to America, where they die in exile and broken-hearted. . . .

"'God Save Ireland,' a selection by the chorus in which the audience joined, closed the entertainment."

International developments also affected McGeeney's literary output. Woodrow Wilson's presidency began in 1913 in high optimism for continued peace. Except for the difficulties in Mexico, foreign affairs played a small role in his early administration. When World War I erupted in Europe in 1914, with Germany and Austria-Hungary aligned against Britain, France, and Russia, the vast majority of Americans believed it would quickly end in compromise. So strong was the sentiment that the United States should maintain its traditional policy of noninvolvement in Old World problems that President Wilson urged his countrymen to be "neutral in thought as well as in action."

Many needs imported from Europe were no longer available, and Americans began making those things themselves. This was true even in motion pictures. Before the war, the big film distributors in the North and East had been having a hard time finding enough pictures to supply the nation's movie houses. To fill their needs, they had brought a large percentage of films from France and Britain. This source was now cut off absolutely.

Not only the big distributors realized that a great number of pictures had to be produced—and quickly. It was known in California and as far south as San Antonio.

There were no movie companies in San Antonio. But McGeeney contended, in the San Antonio *Express,* "There are just as good material and picture players here as anywhere. Within a radius of twenty-five miles every variety of scenery can be found—long rolling plains, desert-like places, deep-shaded woods, hills, valleys and rivers. . . . There need be no delays during the winter period, when in the North and East little outdoor work can be done." With her natural beauty, historical atmosphere, and climatic advantages, the Alamo City should "rank with Los Angeles and New York as a picture-making center."

McGeeney was familiar with movie production. While at San Luis Potosí, he had met and assisted the French director, Gaston Melies, who was in Mexico with his crew to film revolutionary troops and make the first motion pictures of President Díaz. McGeeney had studied Melies' trick techniques. The troop scenes were used in the Melies production, *The Immortal Alamo,* completed at San Antonio in 1911 and starring Francis Ford, older brother of the famous director John Ford, as Davy Crockett.

Gaston Melies, with his brother Georges, represented Star Film, a Paris firm established in the United States in 1904 as an outlet for the French company's products. They began making American films in 1909. After a family split in 1912, Gaston returned to

Theater display, *The Poisoned Pool,* McGeeney's first Lone Star production, filmed on Leon Creek and in Rockhill Club grounds, San Antonio.

A scene from *The Poisoned Pool.*

France, and the U.S. branch continued for a time under the firm name MinA, meaning "Made in America." During his one-year residence in Texas, Gaston Melies had built an elaborate set near San Jose Mission, called Star Film Ranch, where his company made numerous one-reel Westerns, using local cowboys to do the riding stunts and play outlaws and Indians.

The Melies precedent helped McGeeney convince local investors. On September 2, the Lone Star Company was organized "for the production and manufacture of feature films under the Fleur de Lis, 3-C ranch and 4-D ranch brands. . . the scenarios to be written by San Antonio authors, the picture plays to be produced in and about this city and distributed throughout the United States," with the stipulation that "every effort be made to in some way advertise San Antonio in every production sent out from this factory." Named as officers and directors were P.S. McGeeney, president and manager; H.H. Smith, vice-president; Peter O'Brien, secretary-treasurer; Paul O'Brien; and J.J. McManus. The business office was located at 2410 North Flores Street, with studios at Terrell Wells, C.L. Nelson's ranch *(Enceno Solo),* and San Jose, six miles south of the city.

McGeeney was also appointed field representative of *The Mutual Weekly,* the newsreel of the Gaumont Company, "presenting views of the world. . . as timely as a newspaper." Gaumont, a French firm, maintained an office in New York City, where films were imported by George Kleine, a Chicago distributor and leading figure in the motion picture business.

The first Lone Star film was shot on Leon Creek and in the Rockhill Club grounds September 5–6, under the title of *The Poisoned Pool.* "It is a blood-curdling Western," said the San Antonio *Light,* "with plenty of guns and hosses. . . from the pen of P.S. McGeeney, featuring himself in the title role and the best actors and actresses the city affords. . . Miss Evelyn Strahn, Victor Flato, Arthur Hynes, Mrs. Gene Regemy, Miss Florence Scholl, Max Lamm, Tom Anderson, Jack Flaherty and D.A. Weigand. . . . The plot centers around a love intrigue in the desert country; the climax is reached when a rejected lover saves an accepted suitor who, dying from thirst, is about to drink from an arsenic-poisoned water hole."

Determined to produce only the best, McGeeney obtained the services of a Hollywood cameraman, who claimed to be "the very last word in lens craft." After the scenes were shot and the cameraman had departed ("in somewhat of a hurry," thought McGeeney), the film was developed in an old lightproofed barn on North Flores Street, and "thereby we came on the disconcerting revelation that the cameraman was an imposter. While the characters were talking, the camera had been focused on their feet; while they were in the foreground, the lens had been focused on some distant object. . . and the actors seemed to be moving about in a dense fog. There was nothing to do but throw the whole film in a trash can."

The Poisoned Pool retake was by Archer's Art Shop, under McGeeney's direction, and "shown in San Antonio for the first time at the Wonderland Theater, September 21." It ran three days, then was "shown in cities and towns throughout the state. . . . Then a contract was negotiated whereby the picture was transferred to the Sawyer Distributing Company of New York and shown throughout the country."

Later in the year, the San Antonio *Light* announced that "films made in San Antonio are being witnessed by cinematograph audiences in India. . . . According to a letter received from E.H. Ducasse of Calcutta, owner of the Bijou Theater there, *The Poisoned Pool* has been exhibited at the Bijou . . . at the cost of two rupees. . . and received great applause."

Meanwhile, Lone Star produced a four-reel 4-D ranch feature, entitled *The Round Up,* also written by McGeeney. On an even happier note, it landed a contract with the San Antonio Traction Company to make a film depicting the history of the street car service and civic development in the city, allowing Lone Star to "pay its stockholders twenty per cent dividends."

McGeeney titled the work *Helping to Build A City,* and "one thousand feet of film was used in producing the picture." The San Antonio *Express* described it as a "series that begins with a scene in which the street car of 1885, a small, antiquated affair drawn by two little mules, is shown in operation. The driver, serving as both motorman and conductor, meets with a mishap and the car jumps off the rails. Citizens in old-fashioned costumes come to the rescue and finally succeed in replacing the car on the track. The driver reaches the end of the line and, falling asleep on the seat of the car, dreams a wonderful dream of San Antonio's progress.

"In his dream he first sees the mule-car give place to the electric street car of 1895. This antiquated, slow-moving machine is replaced by the larger car of 1905. People marvel at its speed and conveniences. Then comes the modern, 'pay-as-you-go' street car of 1915.

"The latter part of the film shows building development in the downtown section. Street car employees are shown around the offices of business concerns at 'paying-off' time on Saturday afternoon."

Helping to Build A City drew capacity crowds at San Antonio's Empire Theater, Wigwam Theater No. 1, and Pike Theater, where it ran for a week, Monday through Saturday, before being exhibited thoughout the state. At Galveston, Texas, in May 1916, it was used by the Southwestern Electrical and Gas Association in an "anti-jitney" campaign to show the advantages of street car transportation.

With the docu-drama completed, McGeeney began drafting a scenario based on *The Power of Love,* which the San Antonio *Light* noted "is expected to be made into a picture play within 60 days." However, developments involving the United States in the chaotic Mexican Revolution caused him to abandon the project and suspend operations of the Lone Star Company.

Francisco "Pancho" Villa, Mexico's bandit-guerrilla leader and anti-Madero revolutionist, in full regalia.

•11

"Pancho Villa"

American investors saw in General Victoriano Huerta an opportunity to return to the "good old days." President Woodrow Wilson turned a deaf ear and continued his refusal to recognize what he considered "a government of butchers." In 1913 Huerta found himself faced with an uprising of former supporters of Madero and a large party calling themselves the Constitutionalists, led by the ex-governor of the state of Coahuila, General Venustiano Carranza.

In his opus titled "Pancho Villa," McGeeney writes, "Almost every day a revolution was brewing in Mexico. The Mexican people were not happy unless they were quarreling. . . . It would appear that they are all born during the shot and shell of dissension and it was the principal diet on which they thrived."

As the uprising gathered steam, Wilson offered to mediate between the Huerta regime and the Constitutionalists. Both sides rejected his efforts. He next proposed free elections in which Huerta should not be a candidate. In return the United States would encourage American bankers to again extend loans to the Mexican government. Huerta's refusal on August 16 evoked from jingoists a renewed demand for intervention; from Wilson a policy of "watchful waiting" and a strict arms embargo. In October, Huerta dissolved the Mexican Congress and assumed the presidency.

Again Wilson requested Huerta's "retirement" and notified him that it was the policy of the United States to isolate him from material aid and foreign sympathy. In February 1914, Wilson lifted the arms embargo to permit munitions to reach Huerta's opponents. The action was rebuked by Carranza, for whom Wilson then developed a sharp dislike. The president then ordered U.S. naval units stationed off the coast of Veracruz to block the entry of European shipments of war materials to all Mexican factions.

Though Wilson's interference in Mexican affairs undoubtedly stemmed from his belief in the virtues of democracy, it drew fire from Congress. Republicans in the House of Representatives accused him of making the United States the laughingstock of the world.

A precipitate action gave President Wilson a way out of his dilemma. On April 9, several sailors from the U.S.S. *Dolphin,* one of the vessels stationed in Mexican waters, went ashore for supplies and were arrested by Huerta's troops on a charge of violating martial law. They were released promptly, with an expression of regret from Huerta. Rear Admiral Henry T. Mayo, commanding the U.S. fleet, peremptorily demanded a promise to punish the responsible officer and an additional apology by hoisting the American flag on Mexican soil, giving it a twenty-one-gun salute. Huerta declined, unless the Mexican flag were to be saluted in return.

Admiral Mayo made his demands without consulting Washington, but the Wilson administration felt that he must be supported to secure redress of grievances and preclude Huerta from exploiting the incident. Before Congress could act, news was received that a German ship was about to unload munitions at Tampico Bay. Wilson ordered the navy to prevent the delivery and to seize Veracruz.

The city was bombarded and occupied April 21–22, but not in the bloodless way Wilson had wished. Some 300 Mexicans and ninety Americans were killed or wounded. Huerta broke off diplomatic relations with the United States. War with Mexico seemed inevitable.

Argentina, Brazil, and Chile offered to mediate the dispute. With relief, President Wilson sent delegates to confer with Huerta's representatives at Niagara Falls, where in June, the ABC Powers proposed the dictator's resignation, the establishment of a Mexican provisional government favoring agrarian and political reforms, and no indemnity to the U.S. for occupation costs at Veracruz.

Huerta rejected the plan. However, during the summer, his armies were defeated in every part of Mexico. General Carranza entered Mexico City, and Huerta abdicated. The U.S. occupation forces withdrew from Veracruz, their mission of preventing German infiltration into Mexico accomplished. In October 1915, the United States and several Latin American nations recognized Carranza as de facto president.

McGeeney writes, "After billygoat Carranza grabbed hold of the presidential hobbyhorse the Mexican muddle might have ended, if he hadn't broken his promises to Don Pancho Villa." The bandit-guerilla leader and anti-Madero revolutionist, Francisco "Pancho" Villa, had decided in 1913 that it would be in his best interest to join Carranza. In October he had attacked Monterrey in the name of the Constitutionalists but was beaten back by Huerta's forces. A few weeks later he had attacked and overrun the city of Juarez, a victory that made him an important ally. McGeeney writes, "The U.S. recognition of Carranza's government was very distasteful to Villa. He and Carranza quarreled and Pancho started another revolution. Pancho Villa might have won and become president if he hadn't raided Columbus, New Mexico."

During the Huerta regime, small bandit gangs from Mexico constantly had raided farms and ranches on the Texas side of the Rio Grande. Occupied with the Carranza revolt, Huerta did little to discourage the invasions, and residents along the river from Laredo to Brownsville armed themselves to defend lives and property. As the situation grew worse, they appealed to the Texas governor, Oscar B. Colquitt, for help. Governor Colquitt, in turn, called upon Washington to protect the Texas border. But when the Wilson administration suggested that it might be best if the people moved away from the river valley, Colquitt mobilized the Texas National Guard and recruited the Ranger force to full strength. Washington acted at once. Several troops of U.S. cavalry, machine gun units, and artillery were sent to Fort Brown, the Harlingen sector, and as far west as Roma-Los Saenz and Fort Ringgold at Rio Grande City.

The raids increased. During the summer of 1915, railroad tracks were destroyed, trains held up and burned, cavalry ambushed and slain, and many Mexicans killed and captured after local officers and the Rangers chose to overlook orders that the military was not to pursue and shoot at the bandits after they retreated across the river.

Carranza brought a token halt to the plundering across the Rio Grande. But he was unable to control Pancho Villa. In November the little fat man renounced the Constitutionalist Party and declared himself *Jefe* of all Mexico.

Villa roamed at will. Nearly all his followers were from the hills and mountains of Durango and Chihuahua. He hated the wealthy *hacendados* and foreigners; thousands fled the provinces rather than face the *villistas*. He seemed to take pleasure in torturing every Catholic priest who fell into his hands. Priests fled into Texas by the hundreds; a refugee camp was set up on Baffin Bay, near Kingsville, for their housing and safety. So much church property was destroyed that Roman Catholics in the United States urged President Wilson to take drastic action. Wilson would have liked to eliminate both Carranza and Villa, but continued his policy of "watchful waiting."

Villa was brazen. In January 1916, he seized from a train and shot to death sixteen American engineers whom Carranza had invited to return and operate the abandoned mines at Santa Ysabel. On March 9, he raided the border town of Columbus, New Mexico, killing nineteen more American citizens.

The Columbus raid electrified the nation. Congressional pressure for intervention mounted. President Wilson finally acted. With Carranza's reluctant consent, he ordered 6,000 troops under Brigadier General John J. Pershing into Mexico to search out and destroy Villa and his bands.

Pershing entered Mexico in hot pursuit on March 15. By July his troops had moved some 400 miles south through Chihuahua, rarely making contact with the will-o'-the-wisp *villistas,* but clashing instead with Mexican government troops who resented the U.S. intrusion. Pershing also found it difficult to deal with other hostile Mexicans, being under orders from the War Department not to attack any non-followers of Villa who blocked his path. President Wilson had no desire to go to war with Mexico at the same time that U.S. relations with Germany were deteriorating.

McGeeney describes the campaign as "a nightmare of heat,

dust and, when it rained, thick mud. No sight of Pancho. Pershing would have had better luck finding a needle in a haystack. Billygoat Carranza was of no assistance. He couldn't capture Villa himself, but did not want the United States doing it....

"The most noted fight between U.S. and Mexican troops was on the National railroad at Carrizal, where scores were killed and wounded. This situation caused President Wilson to call thousands of National Guardsmen into Federal service to protect the International border."

Army horses and wagons poured into the Expeditionary Force's base of operations at Columbus. Machine gun corps and motor trucks loaded with supplies were rushed into Mexico. The wireless station, the only means of communication with Pershing's troops, hummed day and night. Railroad bridges across the Rio Grande were strictly guarded to prevent any attempts at destruction, and soldiers were quick to respond to any rumor of disturbance.

On July 4, Carranza suggested the appointment of a joint high commission to consider a formula for guaranteeing safety on the border and a U.S. withdrawal. Washington was flooded with telegrams from pacifists urging peace, and again President Wilson accepted compromise.

General Hugh L. Scott, Army chief of staff, arrived in San Antonio to confer on the Mexican situation with Major General Frederick Funston, commanding the Southern Department. Funston announced that hundreds of soldiers were to be "whirled through the city's streets in motor trucks" in a "preparedness parade." He had been "figuring" on the project for some time, but now, perhaps, was staging it primarily for General Scott's benefit.

McGeeney promptly cancelled his tour with *Helping to Build A City* and returned to San Antonio for the action.

Said the San Antonio *Express:* "The Thirtieth Infantry is to be loaded on motor trucks, twenty seven [of them], and hauled fifteen miles. Accounts will be kept on time, gasoline, repairs, damages—all the little points that must be looked to in such tests—and the approximate cost. This is with a view of using trucks for infantry transport in time of war....

"One truck will carry thirty-five men standing and about twenty-eight sitting. Two trucks are supposed to carry one company. The soldiers will be equipped with those articles carried in time of service. . . . It is possible to carry infantry more rapidly than cavalry can march."

Several motion picture representatives were on hand to "get views of the parade," but McGeeney "went into the field" and obtained scenes of "troop loading and unloading." His film, shown at Fort Sam Houston, pleased military authorities. He was issued the following document.

PERMIT TO TAKE MOTION PICTURES

Headquarters Southern Department
Fort Sam Houston, Texas
Aug. 7, 1916

Permission is hereby given to P.S. McGeeney, representing the Gaumont Company, for the period from August 7, 1916, to December 7, 1916, to take motion pictures along the Mexican border, under such conditions and regulations as may be prescribed by the commanding officers, subject to the following provisions:

1. That all plates or films shall be submitted to the said commanding officer and that only such as shall receive his approval shall be published as still photographs separately or shown as motion pictures, the remainder to be left in his possession and to be destroyed.
2. That no films which shall have received the approval of the said commanding officers shall be shown in combination with other motion pictures until such combination shall have received the approval of the War Department.

By command of Major General Funston:
(Signed) Malvern Hill Barnum
Lieut. Col., General Staff,
Chief of Staff

The above permission given at
Headquarters Southern Department,
Fort Sam Houston, Texas, this
7th day of August, 1916.

McGeeney engaged the services of a cameraman, T.T. Dillon, and E.J. Akey, "formerly in the newspaper business at Mission [Hidalgo County] and well known in the Rio Grande Valley."

He named his new enterprise Premier Films, and announced to the San Antonio *Express:* "From Brownsville, Texas, to San Diego, California, in a Saxon automobile, carrying motion picture equipment, we will be grinding out reels of Uncle Sam's fighting forces on the Mexican border. We are steering clear of mere reviews and parades. . . getting real sham battles, charges, etc. Many of them will be real thrillers. Neither will there be any duplication. The automobile has been furnished by the E.H. Labadie Auto Company, Saxon agents here. . . . I am a great admirer of the Saxon-Six and pleased to obtain one for the journey."

The first pictures taken were of the machine leaving the firm's salesrooms. Then a reel was taken of an interview with Major General Funston at Fort Sam Houston, whence the trio departed September 10 for Port Isabel, Texas, "in order that it may be said the trip was made from coast to coast."

The *Express* added: "After reaching San Diego, the party will make the return trip by a northern route, taking views in every State contingent to the border for *The Mutual Weekly*. . . to be released all over the country and even abroad."

McGeeney gives a brief summary of the trek up the Rio Grande and through the Big Bend country. "We filmed most of the different troops and camps under actual war conditions. I had never driven over such rough roads, and in some places there were no roads, simply open country and mountain trails. . . even encountered some bad pits, but these did not hold the Saxon long. The car made light work of heavy going.

"We reached El Paso in October, our journey not half done. The border city, separated by the Rio Grande from the strong Carranzista garrison at Juarez, had assumed a quiet air under its strict military supervision."

The El Paso *Times* reported: "P.S. McGeeney of Premier Films, accompanied by T.T. Dillon and E.J. Akey. . . are guests of R.W. Deason, sales manager of the El Paso Auto Sales company. . . .

"The Saxon-Six which they drove into this city Saturday morning and only weighs 2,300 pounds, tipped the scales at 3,500 pounds. . . . Dillon stated that he was certainly surprised at the way the little car held up under such abnormal road conditions and such a heavy load. From all accounts of the trip the radiator never once boiled over, nor was it necessary to have repair work done at any time.

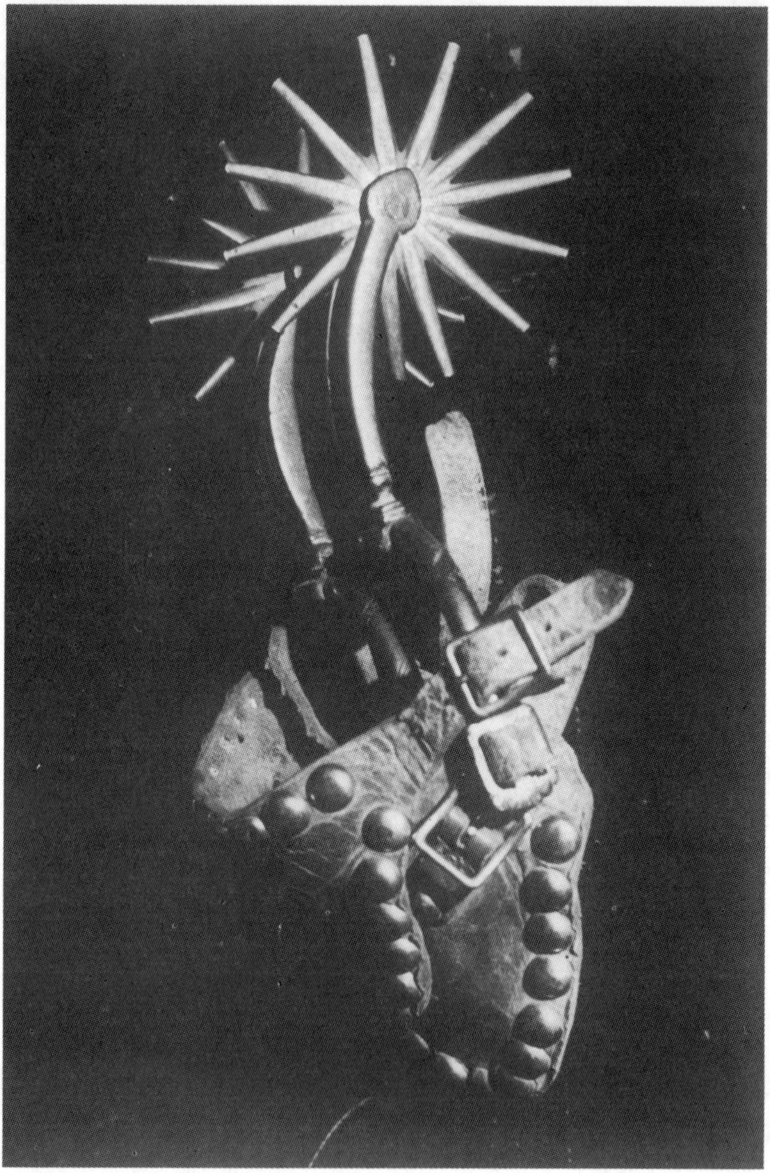

Pair of long-shanked "star" spurs, a gift to McGeeney from Pancho Villa in Mexico (1916).

"Manager Deason has arranged to place this 'wonder car', as he calls it, on exhibition at the Auto Show next week."

The party continued westward, "filming Columbus and the movements of all State militia troops, including the regular army at the forts" along the New Mexico and Arizona borders. They never made it to San Diego. While "making scenes at Nogales," McGeeney secured "endorsement from an aide-de-camp" to cross into Sonora. "Pershing and his troops were still paddling around in Mexico and we intended to join them. The trail was a dim one. As we proceeded farther and farther away from gasoline, oil and water, we decided to turn back. . . lost the trail completely and wandered into the camp of Carranza's erstwhile colleague, Don Pancho.

"We found him laid up with a leg wound. Not a bad fellow at all—that is, if he liked you—but hell on wheels when he didn't. He asked me about Tio Samuel's *soldados,* and many other things. I answered truthfully every question, and he was satisfied. Then he invited us to be his guests—no pictures.

"Before saying *adíos* the next morning, I became interested in his big, long-shanked star spurs, and he gave them to me. He had others, he said. I started to refuse, but I saw a cold gleam in his eyes that spelled murder. With a smile and profuse thanks I took the spurs. When we were ready to hit the road, he sent a man to put us on the right trail to the border.

"This is how I met Pancho Villa."

The joint high commission debated into January 1917. It ruled, among other things, that the American unit commander in the Carrizal affair was at fault, but disbanded without establishing a basis for the withdrawal of American troops. That same month Germany proclaimed unrestricted submarine warfare to prevent the arrival of Allied aid to Britain. In February, U.S. sentiment against Germany was inflamed by the publication of a secret German plan, the Zimmermann Note, for a military alliance with Mexico. President Wilson, who had been reelected on the slogan "He kept us out of war," withdrew the Expeditionary Force and broke off diplomatic relations with Berlin. A new Mexican constitution was proclaimed; Carranza was elected president in March, and the United States extended de jure recognition.

Meanwhile, three American merchantmen were sunk, and Allied shipping losses were so great that Britain's survival was at stake. On April 2, President Wilson asked Congress for a declaration against Germany, calling the U-boat menace "warfare against mankind" and the Allied effort "a crusade to make the World safe for democracy." Congress approved, and the United States was at war in Europe.

And Pancho Villa?

McGeeney concludes, "The Mexican government made a deal with him. . . gave him a ranch, a 1918 Dodge car and fifteen thousand pesos a year to leave its citizens alone. He settled down with his family as an *hacendado* and was doing right well in 1920 when Carranza was assassinated and one-armed General Álvaro Obregón vaulted into the saddle of the bucking presidential hobbyhorse. Then it was announced that the bartender in Madero's old army, Plutarco Calles, was to succeed Obregón as president.

"Pancho saw all colors of the rainbow, for he hated Calles. He put up another candidate. Somebody decided to stop Villa's activities, or thought fifteen thousand pesos was too much money to pay out of the National Treasury every year. . . . Early one morning in July [1923], Pancho and one of his most trusted lieutenants [Miguel Trillo] were ambushed and killed while traveling along the road near Parral, Chihuahua.

"Many people have called Villa a Robin Hood because he fought for the poor. To me, he was the Wes Hardin of Mexico."

•12
Indians I Have Met

In May 1917 Congress passed a selective service act that required all men ages twenty-one to thirty to register for military service, and later included those between eighteen and forty-five. Before the year ended, nearly 200,000 draftees and veterans of the Regular Army were in Europe. Patrick McGeeney, Jr., joined the Navy.

McGeeney himself missed the age limitations in both instances but, with the rest of his family, did his bit at home in Liberty Bond drives, "wheatless Mondays and Wednesdays," "meatless Tuesdays, Thursdays and Saturdays," and "gasless Sundays." He also served on the advisory council of the Motion Picture Industry of the United States, Committee on Americanism. Mary McGeeney responded to Red Cross appeals by knitting woolens for trench-bound soldiers. Twins Jack and Tom were in high school and too young for the service. They helped clean out San Antonio bookshelves to give the soldiers reading matter, and they collected fruit pits, which were saved by the tons across the country and burned to make charcoal filters for gas masks.

McGeeney reorganized the Lone Star Company as the Shamrock Photoplay Corporation, expanded the Terrell Wells facility, and employed N.A. Kent, who had worked in the art departments of Selig, Lasky, and Vitagraph, to "touch up" the San Jose studio for indoor scenes. Said the San Antonio *Express:* "As might be expected of the company that calls itself the Shamrock, with a director by the name of McGeeney, the interior of the studio is green. . . . One end has a stage and rooms where scenery and other properties may be stored, and one-half of the roof has the necessary arrangements of canvas for the diversion of lights. Four twin arc lights are provided so that work may be done under any conditions."

McGeeney kept his cameras cranking. Appearing before a "large gathering" of representative San Antonio businessmen at the Gunter Hotel, he outlined his plans to produce a "spectacular moving picture depicting Texas history from the 16th century to the present, including the great mobilization of the National Guard on the Mexican border." The mayor of San Antonio, county officials, the president of the Chamber of Commerce, leaders of other civic and commercial organizations, and Texas' new governor, James E. Ferguson, "expressed themselves enthusiastically." The production, entitled *The Battle Ground of Nations,* was shown as a part of the two-hundredth anniversary of the founding of the Alamo in the spring of 1918.

In addition, McGeeney presented an "educational picture" showing the "historic and beauty spots" in and around San Antonio, together with the "natural history specimens—elk, buffalo, coyotes, sacred cattle, camels, llamas, Persian sheep, black bears, grizzly bears, deer, mountain sheep, lions, tigers and sea lions—in the Brackenridge Park zoo." Title lines gave the names of the donors.

McGeeney also found time to conduct an "acting school," in which students were taught "film phantasy" (the methods and madness of the film industry); how to determine their adaptability to the movies; how to prepare for the camera (proper make-up, wardrobe, etc.); and how to express emotions from "abashed to yearning." He put his graduates to performing in his own pictures and provided additional opportunity by inviting outside companies to avail themselves of San Antonio's atmosphere, climate, and scenery.

The production genius, Samuel Goldwyn, filming for the Rex Beach Pictures Company of New York, bypassed his handsome studios at Culver City, California, and sent a crew to San Antonio to make *Heart of the Sunset,* based on the popular 1915 Beach novel of that title and starring Robert Tabor, Anna Q. Neilson, and Herbert Hayes. McGeeney served as assistant production manager, obtaining locations and extras, and played a bit part.

Robert Tabor and Anna Q. Neilson in scene from *Heart of the Sunset,* filmed at McGeeney's Shamrock studios in 1918 by Samuel Goldwyn for the Rex Beach Pictures Company of New York.

McGeeney touring Indian reservations, summer of 1919, making documentaries entitled *Indians I Have Met*.

Heart of the Sunset, with the exception of some border scenes shot at Eagle Pass and Del Rio, was completed at the San Jose studio and released by Goldwyn Distributing Corporation of New York in April 1918.

The Rex Beach Pictures Company wrote McGeeney March 2, praising him for his work: "The location, settings and photography are superb, which speak well of the unusual lights in Texas....

"Permit us to thank you for your cooperation with the company that produced the picture and we would ask you to extend our thanks to the people in San Jose for their many kindnesses.

"Should we find it necessary to again send a company to the southwest, we certainly will select San Jose."

McGeeney told the San Antonio *Express:* "Eastern audiences like the West...want to see what they *think* the West is like—cowboys, Indians, Mexicans, bandits and all the complications thereunto pertaining rolled out before them harmlessly on the motion picture screen....I intend to gratify this desire by dishing up the *real* stuff." During the summer, he wrote scenarios and contracted with Ultra Films, Incorporated, of New York for "twelve two-reel features...one finished film to be sent to the company for its approval each month."

For "principal players" he selected "San Antonians who had both stage and screen experience...Guy Robinson and Blanche McGarity, lead characters; Wade Hulette, Angela W. Porter, and Margaret John, supporting characters; Ad Strong, Shelby Terry, and Earl Grayson, heavies; Clara Crandall, vampire roles; Banks L. Miller, Frederick B. Pate, Ethel Pate, and Thelma Kenley, light and heavy dramatic." The initial feature, entitled *Jim of the 3-C Ranch,* was released September 5, 1918; the second, *Down at Apache Pass,* "a story written around the fighting sheriff Pat Garrett, the Apache chief Geronimo, and the notorious Billy the Kid," came one month later; and a third two-reeler, *Down at the 4-D Ranch,* "a story of the Indian Nations as they were before the opening of Oklahoma to white settlement," went to exhibitors on November 5.

McGeeney scheduled, but never completed, the remaining nine features. During an early visit to Ultra Films in New York, he had conferred with President William Steiner of the Jester Comedy Company, "with a view of locating in San Antonio for at least a part of its work." Current Jester releases included *The Recruit,*

His Golden Romance, All "Fur" Her, The Wrong Flat, It's a Great Life, Oh! What a Day, The Fly Ball, and *Ain't It So?* Rights to these comedies had been sold for South and Central America, France, Spain, Portugal, Italy, India, Burma, and Ceylon. This was "big time" to McGeeney. He pointed to the wartime fuel conservation rules which threatened to close many New York studios, and to the fact that San Antonio had "two hours more of antinic [sic] light every day than did New York and one hour more than Los Angeles, an element of great importance to all producers at any time." Too, the Sunset Corporation had established a laboratory at San Antonio, "enabling production companies to develop their test films at once instead of waiting to send them to Los Angeles and other points as was formerly necessary." On September 20, President Steiner decided to take advantage of the Shamrock facilities and San Antonio's climate for his fall and winter activity.

Under the direction of William Seiter, a comedy specialist, the Jester company arrived in San Antonio November 1, announcing that it would "film a series of comedies on a two-a-month basis during the succeeding six months" at Terrell Wells. Its personnel consisted of the great Twede-Dan and Nilde Babette, the famous French actress, for leading parts; Jimmy Aubrey and Pearl Sheppard, both well-known in the comedy field; and A. Rustrelli, remembered by his fans in connection with the "protean acts" of the turn of the century vaudevillian, Mark Linder. These players were supplemented by talent "gathered" by McGeeney for the first Terrell Wells production, *Camouflage,* followed by *Some Baby.*

Movie making news took a back seat, however, as the San Antonio press headlined the war in Europe. It emblazoned the general counterattack by Allied forces that halted the German advance and began the "pushing back" along the Marne. Then came the fall of German-held St. Mihiel on the right back of the Meuse River, the advance through the Argonne Forest, and the bloody victory that cost 177,000 troops killed, wounded, or captured. By November the German armies were in full retreat, the kaiser had been forced to abdicate, and the German provisional government faced imminent collapse. On November 11, before Allied forces could push from France into the Fatherland, representatives of the German army met with Allied represen-

McGeeney touring western United States and Canada, summer of 1919, making a series of documentaries on North American Indian tribes, entitled *Indians I Have Met*.

tatives in a railway car in the Compiegne Forest and signed the armistice that ended more than four years of fighting.

It would be some time before U.S. service men came marching home, and wartime conservation rules remained in effect. The Jester company made eight comedies during the limited period of its contract with Shamrock. President Steiner came to San Antonio to survey the prospects for film production in the area, and "expressed hope it might be made their permanent working place with the exception of such time as might be necessary at other points for the sake of variety." He even envisioned "a motion picture city at Terrell Wells comparable to Universal in California."

Steiner was accompanied by New York director Aubrey M. Kennedy; cameraman Jacob A. "Jake" Badaracco; actors Paul Panzer, Harry Myers, and Robert Tabor (of *Heart of the Sunset*); and actresses Ruth Stonehouse, Edna Holland, Marie Trador, and Blanche Gillespie. Panzer was a veteran of the Boston and New England vaudeville circuits. He had been the hero of several 1912 Pathé Westerns such as *Sing Lee and the Badman, The Sheriff's Brother,* and *The Cowboy and the Baby,* and the villain in the widely acclaimed *Perils of Pauline* (1914). In 1916, he was engaged by the Sunbeam Motion Picture Corporation of Cleveland, Ohio, for the leading role in Sunbeam's first picture, *Hyphenates.* Harry Myers also had appeared in westerns, but would hit his stride in 1922 in the eighteen-chapter Universal serial, *The Adventures of Robinson Crusoe.* Since 1912, Ruth Stonehouse had been the favorite heroine of numerous two- and three-reel productions of Essanay (the George K. Spoor-Broncho Billy Anderson film manufacturing company of Niles, California).

Before his six-month contract with Shamrock expired, Steiner produced a fifteen-episode serial, *The Masked Rider,* starring Myers, Stonehouse, and Panzer. McGeeney again obtained extra players and assisted in the directing and in the camera work of Jake Badaracco.

The Masked Rider was completed at Terrell Wells in May 1919 and sold for distribution to the Arrow Film Corporation of New York. The Steiner contingents departed San Antonio for "the East and West," and McGeeney turned to a "prized project."

An "application to the U.S. government to make educational films of various North American Indian tribes" won approval.

During the summer of 1919, while his family vacationed in Kansas, he "traveled thousands of miles in a Chevrolet automobile" through the western United States and into Canada. His series of documentaries were entitled *Indians I Have Met*. The Christian pastor and best-selling novelist, Harold Bell Wright, wrote McGeeney from Tucson, Arizona, on November 26, "I wish you continued success and consider your project a very valuable contribution to the history of our American people."

McGeeney's summer travels "versed him on the American Indian as well as any other man," and combined with his experiences among the old Oklahoma Territory train robbers and the revolutionary *bandidos* of Mexico, he was well prepared to cross paths again with the Cherokee Indian outlaw, Henry Starr.

•13
A Debtor to the Law

On the basis of a resolution by the Cherokee National Council at Tahlequah and a score of testimonials from officials and friends that Henry Starr had reformed, President Theodore Roosevelt commuted his prison sentence in January 1903. Starr returned to Indian Territory. At the time, he was wanted in Arkansas for the robbery of the Bentonville bank nine years previous, and the state of Arkansas made requisition to the Cherokee Nation for his custody. But the nation refused to extradite in retaliation for Arkansas' past refusal to honor Cherokee requisitions.

Starr worked for a time in a Tulsa restaurant and dabbled in real estate. He married a part Cherokee girl, a schoolteacher, who soon bore him a son, then moved his family on an allotment near Skiatook, where he resided until 1907.

This was the year Oklahoma and Indian territories became a single state. Arkansas authorities had kept the old indictment alive, and a few days after statehood made requisition to Oklahoma's first governor, Charles N. Haskell, for "Starr's person." Governor Haskell rejected the application upon the opinion of the attorney general that there was no authority for extraditing members of the Five Civilized Tribes to a state or territory for a crime less than murder.

Starr did not wait for the attorney general's opinion. He fled to his old haunts in the Osage, teamed up with his former pal, Kid Wilson (recently paroled from the Brooklyn,

Henry Starr on horseback at a ranch near Laredo, Texas, during filming of some of the outdoor scenes in *A Debtor to the Law.*

New York, prison), robbed the bank at Tyro, Kansas of $2,500, and fled to Colorado. At Amity, in Prowers County, they paused long enough to dip into the bank's till for $1,000 and escaped into the mountains.

In the mountains, Starr and Wilson separated. Starr claimed, "Wilson wanted to quit for good. I feared violence at his hands...that he was going nutty." What happened to Wilson remains a mystery in western history.

For months Starr was hunted throughout the Southwest. In Oklahoma, his wife, tiring of his absence and abortive efforts to become respectable, obtained a divorce. In May of 1909, he was captured in Arizona, convicted at Lamar, Colorado, for the Amity robbery, and sentenced to from seven to twenty-five years in the state prison at Canon City.

Starr soon became a trusty in charge of a work gang, studied law in the prison library, and in vindication of his past, wrote his autobiography, *Thrilling Events, Life of Henry Starr,* all of which brought his prison record to the attention of the pardon and parole board. He was paroled in September 1913 with the stipulation that he report once a month and never set foot outside Colorado. He opened a short-order cafe at Holly, in Prowers County, just inside the Colorado line. But people were afraid of the "badman from Oklahoma." Business faltered and Starr vanished. Colorado issued a fugitive warrant for parole violation, and Arkansas revived the bank robbery indictment.

McGeeney read the press dispatches of 1914 while in Kansas promoting *The Power of Love* and raising funds for the Hibernian hospital. "The reports had Starr back in Arizona, and later, in Nevada....Then Oklahoma experienced a series of robberies in which one bank after another was burglarized or had money taken from vaults and counters by disguised bandits led by Starr. The state legislature passed a 'bank robber bill' which authorized the governor to offer a $1,000 reward for the capture of any highwayman or safe blower, dead or alive. This spurred the efforts of officers, but they were unable to capture Henry."

Shortly after nine o'clock Saturday morning, March 27, 1915, Starr and six members of his gang rode into Stroud, Oklahoma, a Lincoln County farming community on the Frisco railroad, fourteen miles northeast of Chandler. One man stayed at the stockyards in charge of the horses. The others split into two groups of three, walked north to Main Street without arousing suspicion, and simultaneously robbed the Stroud State Bank and the First National Bank of currency and silver amounting to $5,800.

It was a feat which the James-Younger gang had attempted at Northfield, Minnesota, and which had cost the lives of the Daltons at Coffeyville. Starr might have been successful, except for the action of a seventeen-year-old schoolboy named Paul Curry. When the robbers left the banks, marching several bank officials and depositors before them, young Curry was standing 150 yards away at his home. As the robbers moved toward their horses, Starr bringing up the rear and shooting in true bandit fashion to clear the street of any opposition, Curry dashed into a meat market nearby. He grabbed up a sawed-off .30–30 Winchester rifle used for killing hogs, ran through the store into the alley, took a position behind some salt barrels, and fired at Starr as he passed.

The heavy slug ripped into the bandit chief's left leg below the hip and brought him down. Temporarily paralyzed about the waist, he tried to return the fire. Curry levered another cartridge into the rifle and threatened to kill him. Starr tossed aside his weapon and surrendered.

The other robbers reached the stockyards and mounted. All escaped except one—Lewis Estes, who was having trouble with his nervous horse. Curry shot him in the neck, breaking his left shoulder and injuring a lung. He was found by a pursuing posse a mile and a half from town, where he had fainted from loss of blood and fallen on the road.

Starr and Estes were carried to the office of Dr. John Evans, who attended their wounds. Neither had anything to say that would help in apprehending their pals; however, three of them were eventually captured at different points in eastern Oklahoma. Two drew short prison terms, and one was acquitted.

Starr and Estes were tried at Chandler. Estes turned state's evidence in exchange for a five-year sentence. Starr pleaded guilty to conjoint robbery and received twenty-five years in the state penitentiary at McAlester. He repeated his prison performance—obeyed the rules, worked in the library, taught classes in spelling and composition to other prisoners, and even assisted the chaplain in his duties. In 1918 Warden A.B. Dick reported that he had "undoubtedly reformed." His leg wound had left him with a permanent limp, and the Lincoln County attorney who had prosecuted him said: "Considering his age and crippled condition, I believe he will bring his career as a bank robber to a close as soon as he regains his freedom." Starr was paroled by Governor J.B.A. Robertson in March 1919.

Again the Arkansas authorities requested extradition. Governor Robertson promptly refused. Starr was safe so long as he remained in Oklahoma.

Starr drifted back to Tulsa, where McGeeney next heard of him. "Several pictures based on the careers of the Daltons, Al Jennings and the James and Younger brothers were being shown around the country. Ex-marshal Bill Tilghman had a picture called *The Passing of the Oklahoma Outlaws,* which included Starr's capture at Stroud. . . . Somebody told Henry he could get rich in the movie business, and he was having an Oklahoma company film his saga."

While San Antonio dreamed of becoming the motion picture center of the Southwest, Tulsa dreamed of becoming a Hollywood-on-the-Arkansas. In March 1912, William Smith, a well-known theater man in Tulsa, bought a $500 movie camera and began making newsreels of local events and characters. A second venture launched in 1913 featured the city and six girls chosen to play the part of "pilgrims," and was managed by E.N. Adams, assistant secretary of the Commercial Club, as a civic enterprise. Two years later, a company under the guidance of H.A. Mackle acquired use of the International Dry Farming Congress grounds near Lewis Avenue and the Frisco tracks for making pictures. Tulsa was chosen, Mackle said, because of its "different" scenery and "superior" climatic conditions. By 1919 movie making in Tulsa was on a more permanent basis, with studios and a regular western street of false fronts on the Sand Springs Road. *The Wrecker, The Cowboy Ace,* and several other features were made before a fire put the studios out of business in 1922. The industry ended with William Smith's untimely death in 1925.

Early in 1919 the Pan-American Motion Picture Company of Tulsa was organized and given a permit by the state to sell $120,000 worth of stock. Henry Starr contracted with the company for the story of his life. In November, producer W.C. Martin sent a film crew to Stroud to carefully reconstruct the most spectacular bank robbery in Oklahoma history.

The same bank buildings were used and the busy Saturday afternoon traffic was depicted. Not all the original characters were available—most of the Starr gang was behind bars. Portraying himself with vim and vigor, Starr lined up the bank employees, and the townspeople reenacted the scenes, even down to the wounding and capture of the bandit leader by Paul Curry, who had returned from the war with a Distinguished Service Decoration for bravery in action in France.

The Pan-American company ground out hundreds of feet of film, only to discover "the lighting was all wrong." Director George Rhems appealed to the Shamrock studios at San Antonio. According to McGeeney, "his cameraman lacked considerable expertise, and Rhems wanted me to remake most of the picture."

McGeeney met Rhems at Muskogee, southeast of Tulsa. With the exception of Henry Starr and a man named George Smith who had been hired to furnish a bunch of cow ponies, all those present were movie people. Starr was well-dressed, a man of fine appearance—"more handsome an Indian" than McGeeney had remembered him. Their meeting that "memorable night" at Ponca station was not mentioned. Starr seemed surprised that McGeeney was in the motion picture business, but had no objection to his filming the story.

A story line was lacking. The Stroud banks and street scenes made in outdoor light, McGeeney determined, could be salvaged and "dramatic highlights" of the bandit's life "woven in." The two men "chatted into the night." The world already knew about his escapades, Starr said; he wished people to understand the "true basis" for his actions.

McGeeney continues, "Starr began with his birth in the Cherokee Nation, forty-six years before. . . . He was an honest boy. His dream was to become a rancher. He reached young manhood with the spirit of thrift in him . . . worked with diligence for several cattle outfits and saved his wages. 'Firewater' he passed up.

"In time he secured a small tract of land and a small herd of cows and had a few dollars in the bank. When his own ranch did not need his services, he would work for others. Some of his neighbors became jealous of his success and cunningly planned to beggar him.

"In those days the Indian nation was a wild, unruly country. Criminals from hither, thither and yon took up abode there. The scant law and order was maintained by a few deputy United States marshals—good men, but some of them were worse than the outlaws they were supposed to bring to justice. Their only compensation was derived from fees. I served as a deputy so I can speak with some authority about those stirring times when men were HE and wrist watches were not.

"One day a neighbor Starr was working for asked him to go to town for the mail and some supplies. Henry hitched a couple of broomtails to a light spring wagon and drove away. He had traveled about two miles on his journey when two men carrying a black traveling bag came out of the timber alongside the road. Surmising that they were going to town, he invited them to ride with him.

" 'Pardner, if it's all the same to you,' one of the men said, 'take this bag into town and give it to "Curley." It will save us the trip.'

"Everybody knew Curley, a small restaurant owner. Without hesitation, Henry told them to put the bag under the seat, and drove off dreaming of the day he would become a big cattleman.

"As he approached town, his reveries were rudely interrupted. Two mounted deputy marshals blocked his path.

" 'Who are you? Where are you going' one asked.

" 'Henry Starr. I'm going to town for the mail and supplies.'

"The deputy gave his partner a knowing glance. 'What have you got in that bag?'

" 'I don't know,' Henry replied. 'A couple of fellows about four miles back put it in the wagon and asked me to take it to Curley.'

" 'Let's see what's inside!' the deputy commanded.

"Henry took the bag from under the seat, placed it on his knees and opened it. Dumfounded, he gazed from the contents to the faces of the marshals. 'Whiskey!' he exclaimed.

" 'Right you are!' The deputy grinned.

" 'B-but it's not mine,' stammered Henry.

"Nonetheless, transporting liquor into the Indian Nations was a felony and possession nine points of the law. Henry was placed in leg irons and taken to jail. His heart heavy, and in silence, he endured the trip. When the prison door clanged behind him, he sank upon the rude bunk and yielded to his sorrow.

"Sleep did not come during the long, lonely night. He asked the jailor who brought him his meager breakfast what the law intended to do with him.

" 'You'll be tried when the court convenes,' came the reply.

" 'When will that be?' Henry asked.

" 'In two or three months. I'll send you a lawyer. Maybe he can get you out on bond.'

" 'Get him!' said Starr, hope entering his breast.

"Henry related simply the events leading to his arrest. 'You're in a bad fix,' said the lawyer, his forehead wrinkling into a frown. 'You were caught with the goods, and I'm afraid the judge will take the marshals' word against yours. I will take your case, but I must have a retainer fee. Have you any money or property?'

"Henry gave him a full account of his financial condition. The lawyer wasn't satisfied.

" 'The court fees and my retainer will exceed your cash in the bank. Your cattle, I believe, will be enough collateral to secure a bond.'

"Poor innocent Henry, unwary of the ways of the white man, exclaimed: 'Take it all! Just get me out of here!'

" 'I'll do my best,' promised the lawyer.

"He returned in the afternoon with a legal document, which he read to Henry. Starr agreed to all the conditions without hesitation, and the jailor witnessed his signature. Henry and the lawyer left the jail together. . . . About ten days later, Henry was advised that his case had been dismissed.

"Starr brooded over his loss and social disgrace. Bitter thoughts about the two men who had placed the satchel of whiskey in the wagon never left his mind. He did not seek revenge by taking their lives, Indian though he was. He respected God's commandment 'Thou shalt not kill!' He sought them to clear his good name, without finding them. He tried to find contentment by starting over again, but cruel Fate was marshaling her unconquerable forces. . . .

"During a poker game and drinking bout engaged in by the arresting deputies and shyster lawyer, they boasted how they had bilked the young Indian out of his cows and hard earned money. The boast reached Henry's ears, and he saw red. . . . Despair entered his soul, and drove him to a life of crime.

"During his long career as an outlaw but one man bit the dust from the bark of his gun. He had killed Deputy Marshal Floyd Wilson in self-defense, he said, and regretted the taking of that life."

Henry Starr (arms folded), McGeeney (with badge and rifle), William Karl Hackett (in plaid shirt), and other unidentified members of Pan-American Motion Picture Company cast and film crew in *A Debtor to the Law.*

In a scene from *A Debtor to the Law* Deputy Marshal Wilson (McGeeney) learns that Henry Starr (Hackett) was last seen on Wolf Creek, Cherokee Nation.

Though willing to accept Starr's version as the correct one, McGeeney did not wish to place a premium on crime or make a hero out of an outlaw. His purpose, he told Starr, was to "bring out a moral—to show the fairminded what greed will do to men who have lost their Christianity." Starr assented, but thought it "risky" to leave Oklahoma in light of the Arkansas indictment.

McGeeney had a solution. He slipped Starr aboard the train carrying George Smith and his cow ponies. The costumes and props were packed into trunks and shipped on a separate train with Rhems and his performers.

To avoid publicity about his presence in San Antonio, Starr was kept under wraps at the Gunter Hotel and appeared "incognito" when needed as advisor. His role was played by William Karl Hackett, a twenty-six-year-old Missouri native, formerly of Selig fame, brought to Texas by McGeeney to appear in westerns. McGeeney assisted with directing and camera work and played the role of Starr's nemesis, Deputy Marshal Floyd Wilson—shot to death while trailing the Starr gang following the Missouri-Pacific railway station safe robbery at Nowata.

George Smith, in a letter written October 11, 1965, recalled, "Henry and I had a room in the Gunter on the mezzanine floor overlooking the lobby. . . could see everything and everybody who came and went. We didn't get up until noon, and just signed tickets for our meals, at the barber shop, cleaning shop, tobacco counter—where anybody would take them. . . .

"I got real well acquainted with Henry and he told me a lot about his robberies. . . . He was also quite a gambler. One night he borrowed $20 from me and came in about 2 A.M., woke me up and said, 'Look at my leg.' He had on long underwear and his socks pinned to it with safety pins. Wrapped around his leg inside the underwear was $1,000 in poker winnings, and he gave me a hundred dollar bill.

"We were at the hotel about three weeks. We made one trip to Mexico [Laredo] where some of the outdoor scenes were made, and were guests at a couple of ranches. . . . I felt sorry for Henry. He said that if he didn't make a lot of money out of the picture, he didn't know how to make a living; because of his crime record nobody would hire him. He liked the border country, and thought about buying an airplane, light near some town and steal a car, rob the bank and fly into Mexico."

The filming at Terrell Wells was completed in early December. Starr was pleased with the production and presented McGeeney with a .45 Bisley Model Colt revolver. The Pan-American crew entrained for Oklahoma. Starr returned with Smith and his ponies. Arkansas authorities did not know he had been out of Oklahoma until the picture was released to exhibitors. It was titled *A Debtor to the Law.*

Henry became the hero of a second Pan-American offering entitled *Evening Star.* In both cases his contracts were on a percentage—if the films didn't make money, he didn't get paid. The profits from *A Debtor to the Law,* he claimed, amounted to $15,000. He got only promises. He was advised to hire a lawyer, but he had little respect for lawyers and could not afford the fees. He pleaded for a few hundred dollars from old friends, and kept warring with W.C. Martin.

George Smith recalled his last visit with Starr late in 1920. "He had received nothing from his pictures. I'm sure the pictures lost quite a bit of money. . . too much expense, and they weren't very popular. When Henry left me, he said, 'I imagine that the next time you hear from me I will be dead.' And of course that is what happened."

On February 18, 1921, Starr, with three confederates, tried to rob the bank in Harrison, Arkansas. Starr had scooped up $6,000 when the sixty-year-old former president of the bank stepped from the vault with a rifle and shot him in the ribs and spine. His confederates escaped. Starr died three days later.

•14
Little Miss Bluebonnet

A family tragedy caused McGeeney to suspend his Shamrock operations in early 1920. Patrick, Jr., back from the navy, was visiting his grandmother in Newton, Kansas. The evening of February 1, an open gas stove exploded, setting the 1002 Ash Street residence in flames and severely burning Elizabeth McGeeney "about the face, neck, arms, hands, and body." Patrick helped rush her to the Bethel Hospital, where she died at 5:30 A.M., February 2, aged seventy-three.

The probate of her estate sharply divided the surviving members of the family. McGeeney, for the first time, became aware of what had been transpiring (as he termed it) behind his back. The bachelor uncle, Pat, in his last will and testament made several years before his death in 1914 at Deming, New Mexico, had devised and bequeathed to his bachelor nephew, Michael, Jr., all his "monies and property of every nature and description and wherever situated (chiefly a block of lots and the Ash Street home in Newton)," upon the understanding that Michael should "take care of and support his mother and sisters during their lifetime." To Patrick Sylvester and Edmund L. McGeeney, he left "each one dollar." When Michael's death removed him from the picture in 1911, a codicil devised and bequeathed the properties to Elizabeth McGeeney.

All might have gone well, except that Elizabeth had decided to "carry out the intentions" of Uncle Pat.

In her last will and testament made at Newton in July 1917,

she bequeathed to Mary Winifred Harrison, "all my household furniture, goods and personal effects of every nature and description. . . the house, barn and surrounding lots (16, 18, 20, 22, 24, 26 and 28, Block 15 of the city of Newton), [and] if such house and lots are sold, she to have the proceeds thereafter or as hereafter invested for her." All remaining lots in Block 15 (1 through 17, 19, 21, 23, 25, and 27) she devised and bequeathed to Mary Harrison and Elizabeth Jane Chapman, "they to share and share alike therein, or same to be sold and the proceeds divided equally between them, [and] if same are sold before my death, the proceeds or reinvestment to be their joint property unless divided by me or otherwise disposed of. . . . Unto my two sons, Patrick S. McGeeney and Edmund L. McGeeney, do not give any of my property. . . for they are much better able to care for themselves than their said sisters, and I think they will understand and appreciate the same."

Edmund's reaction is not known. He seldom visited from Colorado, and upon his death was buried at La Junta. The sisters hardly approved of Patrick Sylvester's "wild schemes," and Elizabeth McGeeney apparently had felt that any estate share given him would quickly vanish in his movie enterprises at San Antonio. For whatever reason, McGeeney visited Newton on few occasions thereafter.

He took solace in other family matters during the months to come. His son Jack graduated from high school in January 1921. In father's footsteps, Jack found employment with an oil company in Tampico, Mexico. Tom graduated in May and joined his twin. Patrick, Jr., became a sales representative for a Texas firm and married a Victoria girl, who soon bore him a daughter, Mary Louise. His work eventually took him to Alaska, thence California, and Mary McGeeney spent much of her time with Patrick's family in Victoria.

"Pretty much alone" that summer, McGeeney wrote several scenarios in anticipation of "a big year in film making." His plans were interrupted by the disastrous San Antonio flood of September 1921.

Texas weather, because of the state's great elevation differences and peculiar geographic position between the high plateau of the Rocky Mountains and the Gulf of Mexico, is marked by very rapid changes and extremes in temperature. Droughts, hurricanes, tornadoes, and turbulent thunderstorms accompanied by hail had been the concern of early explorers, missionaries, Anglo-American colonists, military posts, and settlements from the time that the bureaucratic Spanish officials began to keep records. The heaviest thunderstorms in Texas history occurred in the counties north of Bexar on September 6–10, dumping from seventeen to thirty-six inches of rain over thousands of square miles in a two-day period. Damages were estimated at $17,000,000, and 224 lives were lost in the resulting floods. The San Antonio River swept out of its banks, devastating much of the city.

Scenes taken by news weeklies and shown in theaters throughout the country, as well as graphic accounts in the press, gave a fairly accurate impression of the extent to which the city suffered. Little national publicity, however, was given to the complete restoration of the devastated areas made in relatively short time by San Antonians imbued with the spirit which had made heroes of Colonel William Barret Travis' handful of men at the Alamo.

McGeeney was one of the "animated" workers who helped "remake" the city, and spent weeks assuring his contacts in the East and North that his Shamrock facilities had suffered little damage and were still available. In December he leased his Terrell Wells studio to the Neal Hart Production Company.

In 1921 Neal Hart was one of the country's most popular Western stars, touted by his producers and exhibitors as "America's Pal." He was born Cornelius Augustus Hart, Jr., in Richmond, New York, in 1879. His father, former auditor of the city of New York, could well afford to indulge his adventurous offspring in western vacations. At age fourteen, Neal worked on a horse ranch on the Sioux reservation in South Dakota. At age sixteen, he took a job freighting supplies from Ft. Pierre to Rapid City in the Black Hills, then rode with a trail herd into Rawhide Buttes, Wyoming.

In 1896, deciding that an education would give him a better handle on life, Neal enrolled at Bucknell University in Lewisburg, Pennsylvania. When his schooling was interrupted by the Spanish-American War, he enlisted in the navy and served on the U.S.S. *Panther.* After the war, he returned to Bucknell and earned a degree in civil engineering. His degree took him to the Adirondacks of Pennsylvania as superintendent of construction on the Thurman branch of the Delaware and Hudson Railroad, thence to Titusville with the Titusville Electric Traction Company, and finally to the Galesburg and Kowanee railroad in Illinois.

Again the West beckoned, and Neal headed for Wyoming. During the next few years he worked on ranches around Big Pines and served briefly as city marshal and deputy sheriff at Manville, where he was credited (by studio publicity) with "breaking up a band of rustlers who terrorized [neighboring] Converse County." True or not, he certainly learned the rudiments of good roping and horsemanship on the Big Pines ranches, became a star performer for the famed Miller Brothers 101 Ranch Wild West Show in 1907, and like many other 101 cowboys, gravitated from the sawdust arena to the back lots and movie ranches of Hollywood as an expert rider/stuntman and extra.

Director George Marshall of Universal Pictures saw in Neal the "little something" that the public fancied and gave him minor roles in a trio of 1916 featurettes. When the war erupted in Europe, with Mexican bandits raiding along the U.S. border, Neal had the further distinction of appearing in *Liberty, A Girl of the U.S.A.*—a "preparedness" serial starring cliff-hanger heroine Marie Walcamp and Jack Holt and Roy Stewart, both destined to become major western stars. In 1917 Neal signed a one-year contract with Universal for a series of "Mustangers"—perhaps the best of Universal's western shorts, which also stampeded Harry Carey, Art Acord, Jack Hoxie, Pete Morrison, and other cowboy actors to success in the 1920s.

When Neal's contract expired, Universal seemed not to know what to do with him. He hadn't been exactly a runaway success. His performance was acceptable, but these "oaters" followed a strict formula and lacked the fast-paced action to show off his athletic prowess. He had learned his trade well under George Marshall, who, without intending to, had taught him the fundamentals of writing and directing. In 1918 he set up shop in his familiar haunts of Wyoming, where he wrote, directed, and starred in his own production, *When the Desert Smiled. Desert* promptly sold to the Arrow Film Corporation, and Neal Hart was on his way to stardom.

During 1919 he turned out a long series of two reelers for the Chicago-based Capital Film Company, which also released the output of the companies formed by Helen Gibson, ex-outlaw Al Jennings, Lester Cuneo, and Texas Guinan. When the Capital series was completed in 1920, Pinnacle Productions of Glendale, California, signed him for a half-dozen five-reel features released through the Independent Film Association. These features, crammed with thrills and adventure, won Hart a matinee audience who would remain loyal over a decade.

In 1921 Hart organized his own company to produce full-length westerns. He associated himself with William Steiner (now marketing several good series of independent features in America and abroad), enlisted Jake Badarraco as photographer, and signed on Paul C. Hurst (who became Monte Hale's sidekick at Republic in the mid-1940s) to assist in directing and writing adaptations. Hart liked the scenery of Canada and the Northwest Mounted Police. In his first Steiner release, *Tangled Trails,* he is Corporal Jack Borden, who pursues a murderer from Canada to New York, then back to the Northwest, and finally "gets his man."

Hart also liked the Texas border country, and came to San Antonio to film five western features "on location." His cast included William Quinn, Hazel Maye, Sarah Bindley, Max Wesell, and Ben Corbett.

McGeeney had an affinity for the five-foot nine-inch, 170-pound, brown-haired, blue-eyed Neal Hart—quiet, gentlemanly, witty in a dry way, but quick to launch into memories of the early days. Both men had served as peace officers and railroad construction superintendents, and had lifted themselves by their own bootstraps to a successful niche in the movie industry. Too, Hart was Catholic, and had a young son named Tom.

McGeeney suggested several revisions in Hart's scripts. Hart not only graciously accepted the changes, but also gave McGeeney a minor role in the first feature filmed at San Antonio, *Rangeland.*

According to McGeeney's version of the plot, Ned Williams (Hart), an ex-cowboy turned deputy sheriff, incurs the wrath of his arch enemy Bud Spaugh (Max Wesell) by arresting two of Spaugh's men for tampering with a neighboring rancher's cattle. Spaugh blames the rustling on a stranger in the area. The "rustler," when captured by Ned, turns out to be Betty Howard, a forlorn little girl who steals to keep her sisters and brothers from starving. This in no way accounts for the number of cattle that are missing, however. Ned becomes attached to the little girl.

When she tries to help him, Spaugh frames Ned with a holdup and kidnaps the girl. Ned escapes, rescues the girl, and in a desperate fight in the lava beds makes Spaugh his prisoner. Spaugh confesses to being the leader of the real thieves.

The role of Betty Howard was played by San Antonio's golden-haired beauty queen and McGeeney protege, Blanche McGarity.

Rangeland was completed in January 1922, followed by *Heart of A Texan,* in which McGeeney also played a bit part. The three remaining five-reelers, *Lure of Gold, West of the Pecos,* and *Table Top Ranch,* were finished in April, and the Neal Hart company left Texas to make *Butterfly Range,* based on incidents from Hart's days as a deputy sheriff in Wyoming.

Before the company departed, vaudeville actress Grace Cameron, a long-time McGeeney acquaintance on tour with Loew in *Little Dolly Dimples,* appeared at the Princess Theater in San Antonio. McGeeney arranged to produce her stage play as a motion picture. The *Evening News* noted, "The story deals with orphan life, with Miss Cameron in its midst, the center of which filming will be a local orphanage."

Work on *Dimples* began in May. Miss Cameron was "supported by a cast of San Antonio men, women, boys and girls." Several historical and beauty spots in the city "got into the picture," and a "large ballroom scene" was filmed in the Gunter Hotel.

Dimples was immediately followed with *Little Madcap,* directed by McGeeney and released as a Poppie Perfect Picture, bearing the trademark of a red and white poppy flower. Ricord Gradwell, president of Producers Security Corporation, New York, wrote McGeeney on July 12, "I would have recognized your signature and letterhead without the flower. . . . I don't know that your change to the poppy is a good one."

But McGeeney already had discarded the poppy for the bluebonnet (*el conejo,* the rabbit), adopted as the state flower in 1901 by the legislature at the request of the Society of Colonial Dames of America in Texas.

While working on *Dimples* and *Madcap,* he was invited to confer with the City Club, an organization of movers and shakers bent on correcting the erroneous impression among people in the East and North that the metropolis had been "drowned" in the 1921 flood. Much had been proposed, but little accomplished.

McGeeney suggested a motion picture embracing all the grand

McGeeney, Neal Hart, and Blanche McGarity in a scene from *Rangeland,* the first of the Neal Hart western features filmed by William Steiner Productions at San Antonio (1922).

Babe Ruth of the New York Yankees and Blanche McGarity at League Park, San Antonio, choose sides by the time-honored method of putting one hand over another on a bat. Scene from *Little Miss Bluebonnet,* a McGeeney production of April-June 1922.

old landmarks of the city and the new, better and more attractive features that had replaced some less desirable sections since the deluge. It would not be a so-called "commercial" and "propaganda" film as had been made in the past, but a travelogue in which "some of the rich history of more than 200 years accumulation is narrated . . . a thread of romance running through it to make it sufficiently interesting to the theater going public everywhere." The cast would be made up principally of San Antonio's capable artists. Public figures would appear as themselves. Other characters in the story would be portrayed by Hispanics dressed as Indians.

And who should be cast as star and narrator? Why, if possible, San Antonio's own answer to Mary Pickford—little, demure, golden-haired Blanche McGarity.

Hadn't Blanche won first place among 50,000 participants in the Brewster Fame and Fortune Contest of 1919 as the most promising in talent and most beautiful girl in America? She was an experienced actress and Texas born—of hardy stock and the same indomitable spirit and high courage which distinguished her ancestors. They had been pioneers, Irishmen, fighters. The name of her great-uncle, Jesse McCoy, was graven on the tablets of honor in the Alamo. She was "truly a girl for the part."

Miss McGarity consented. The City Club bore the expense of the project. McGeeney titled the film *Little Miss Bluebonnet,* and "rushed it to completion in order to take advantage of the flowers already abloom in profusion."

Little Miss Bluebonnet exemplifies McGeeney's best scripting and directing. Together with the performance of the winsome, naive Blanche McGarity, it deserves more than passing mention.

In an introductory scene, Little Bluebonnet and her pony Tipperary—"Tip" as she calls her inseparable companion—romp among the sun-kissed hills overlooking her beloved San Antonio. Through the golden haze of evening they return home, the little Irish girl's arms laden with the sapphire-hued blooms of her namesake. She tenderly clasps the flowers to her breast; a smile of contentment makes radiant her lovely features as she surveys the great open spaces in the gathering dusk. In the distance, a Spanish mission is silhouetted briefly against the sky and disappears in the coming darkness. To the left, the far-flung skyline of the city gives way to the myriad lights of the canyons of com-

Autographed photo of Blanche McGarity, San Antonio's golden-haired beauty queen and McGeeney protege.

merce, flickering like fireflies in the velvety night.

Little Bluebonnet caresses the head of her pony and whispers in his ear, "Tip, old pal, it makes me happy to show our Eastern friends the beauties of our historic city, where the sun always shines and God's great outdoors reflects His infinite goodness. Do you understand?"

Tip nods knowingly. Slowly the scene fades as Little Bluebonnet continues whispering in Tip's ear.

The story begins at the Southern Pacific railway depot, where several people await the arrival of the New York express. Apart from the group stands Little Bluebonnet, modishly attired, distinctly beautiful. Eagerly, expectantly, her eyes follow the shining ribbons of steel into the middle distance, into which suddenly looms the giant locomotive. With a little cry of pleasure, she steps forward to meet a polished, handsome young man who alights from the cars, followed by two girls. The young man is George Derrington, a New York banker (San Antonio actor J. Herbert Peairs). The two girls are his sisters—friends of Little Bluebonnet who have come to visit. She greets them with a gentle courtesy; for Derrington, it is love at first sight. They are whisked away in an automobile, Little Bluebonnet telling how she is going to honor them with a personally conducted tour of the city's spots of beauty and hallowed associations.

They lunch at the Gunter Hotel, after which the party visits an automobile show at the St. Anthony, Bluebonnet driving a new car down Peacock Alley.

She takes them to the Alamo, where two soldiers clad in the gray of the "Lost Cause" tirelessly patrol the walls. As they stand reverently before the Cradle of Texas Liberty, Little Bluebonnet relates briefly the noble sacrifice of the brave souls who fought to the death for their ideals in those spring days eighty-six years previously. Derrington notes a quaver in her voice as she numbers her own antecedents among the glorious dead. He sees, too, the glint of sunlight in her hair and vows he never realized that the sheen of silk and the shimmer of gold could be merged so beautifully. As they turn to leave, he is taken aback by Little Bluebonnet's admiring glance and thrown into confusion.

Through winding streets and ways the party reaches the missions, one by one. At each mission, Little Bluebonnet gives the date of its erection, graphic bits of history, and describes the privations the missionaries must have endured in establishing these outposts of civilization so that "heathen" children might know the Gospel.

At Concepción Mission, they witness a band of "savages," stripped to the waist and armed with ancient weapons, storming the portals. One of the Indians, pursued, rushes up to the door and calls to be rescued. A portly priest appears, carrying a crucifix, and the Indians prostrate themselves in obediance. The Indians depart in peace; school children come out to play; and the priest walks among them.

At San Jose, the famous window carved by Huicar by special order of the king of Spain is featured. Thence, Little Bluebonnet leads them to the famous old aqueduct south of the city, built in decades past to carry water to flocks grazing in the river valley.

Returning on the high road, Bluebonnet and her friends take a final survey of the landscape dotted with small Mexican settlements. The love-light of homeland in her eyes, she indicates numerous points of progress with her pink little hand, which Derrington follows assiduously. Her healthy color is heightened by her enthusiasm—or is it because of the handsome New Yorker's flashing glances?

Another day dawns. Squirrels disport themselves and songbirds twitter as Bluebonnet and her friends wend their way through serpentine avenues of trees to the heart of the winter playground of the Southwest—Brackenridge Park. The road commences a steep, tortuous incline, with some wonder of Nature at every turn. They reach the summit of Alpine Drive and pause on the brink of San Antonio's fairyland—the Japanese Sunken Gardens.

Miniature lakes smile at the blue sky and reflect white clouds in their depths. Huge lily pads float on the placid waters. Rustic bridges span the narrows, and meandering paths lead to secluded retreats where stone benches and nooks in the rocky walls invite with blue shadows. Across the basin, Derrington sees the "Tea Room," a masterpiece of Japanese architecture. His eyes travel over the lagoon set in a wealth of color afforded by the greatest variety of flowers imaginable. Never has he seen heavier foliage relieved by the scarlet of poppies, which in turn give way to the yellow and purple and black of modest pansies, with the blue of hyacinths dominating all. Yet, reflects Derrington, it cannot rival the lapis lazuli of the eyes of Little Bluebonnet.

She calls him from his reverie. "Shall we see the winter sports of San Antonio?" He assents reluctantly.

On the way out of Brackenridge Park they pause at the municipal golf links. Bluebonnet informs her friends, "This is the course on which Bob McDonald won the largest purse ever offered in America at a professional tournament." She is invited to take a few strokes, but demurs. Derrington urges. Is she not a girl of the great outdoors, equal to any occasion? With a dazzling smile, Bluebonnet acquits herself admirably. Is Derrington a fan? Yes, quite a fan!

So Bluebonnet and her guests proceed to League Park, where the New York Yankees are in training. All the Yank celebrities seem to be on hand, including Babe Ruth; upon the appearance of Bluebonnet and her party, a ball game is arranged and a plot hastily concocted to involve Bluebonnet in its toils. She and Babe Ruth "choose sides" by the time-honored method of putting one hand over another on a bat. Derrington's object of adoration is next seen in the pitcher's box, "striking them out." Bluebonnet shows admiration for the mighty Ruth, whom Derrington keeps under a baleful eye. He suppresses a sigh of relief as they leave the park. Bluebonnet pretends not to notice.

Playfully she reminds her friends, "We have not yet taken our plunge." They frolic at one of the popular bathing beaches, where Bluebonnet—much to Derrington's edification—proves herself a graceful mermaid.

She then promises her guests a "real diversion," and they make their way to Medina Lake, that turquoise gem nestling in the heart of the Bandera Hills some thirty miles west of San Antonio. Here Bluebonnet teaches them Izaak Walton's fine art by landing a goodly fish.

Bluebonnet's little black and white pony has not been forgotten. The scenes are interspersed with Tip and his mistress cantering over the rolling country. In the distance are hundreds of cattle. She pets her pal and tells him of the things she is doing. Tip shakes his head wisely, and she is convinced that the course she is pursuing is right.

Finally, Bluebonnet and her friends arrive at Fort Sam Houston and are greeted by the stately commandant himself, Major General John L. Hines. General Hines, accompanied by a retinue of other officers stationed here, shows them the old gray walls of the Quadrangle, the Campanile, and the cantonments which housed so many of America's sons in training during the Great War. Before leaving, Bluebonnet—to Derrington's dismay—shakes hands with the general, then makes a surprising announcement. "Did you know that I have been invited to lead the grand march with General Hines at the Queen's Ball tonight? As my guests, I trust that I may have the pleasure of your company." Her friends are happy to go, but, thinks Derrington, "to deuce with the General."

The military ball, a highly formal affair given at the Elks Club in honor of the army officers at San Antonio, is shown. Many distinguished heroes of the World War participate. It is a memorable night for Derrington. How brilliant the pageant! And how wondrously sweet Little Bluebonnet as she looks in awe at the queen! "But the queen is not one-half so beautiful as you," Derrington remarks, and Bluebonnet's eyes drop as she modestly accepts the compliment.

After the grand march, Derrington claims Bluebonnet from the general. Instead of dancing, he leads her out into the patio, flooded with silvery light from the moon riding high in the heavens. A soft breeze stirs the fronds of the palms overshadowing the garden seat to which he leads the girl of his dreams. He talks of the events of the past two days. Then, all semblance of embarrassment vanished, he asks the great question. Bluebonnet turns away, gazing steadfastly into the night.

In fancy, she sees her dear Tipperary, her pal of carefree days. Tip winks and shakes his head in the negative. The fancy fades.

Bluebonnet turns back to Derrington. The compassion in her voice is lost as she pronounces doom to his proposal.

Derrington is stunned. Could she not give her heart because it belonged to another?

"I could never be satisfied in your great city," she states, simply. "Tip needs me. My heart belongs to Texas and San Antonio."

The segment dims and resolves itself into the introductory scene. Little Bluebonnet, her arms laden with the flowers of her namesake, stands beside her pony. She smoothes his mane, presses her face against his—whispers in his ear, "And so—I am with you for always."

Tip tosses his head, happily.

McGeeney sent his film to Chicago for development and

trimmed the picture to two reels. At a private showing before the City Club, the "enthusiasm of the directors knew no bounds." The local press commended it as the "most complete motion picture ever made of San Antonio." It "scored heavily" at its first showing at the Rialto Theater during the week of June 19.

McGeeney then sent the picture "back North," where it was "turned into thirty-two prints" and forwarded to "educational distributing stations. . . ultimately to reach every town with a movie house in the country."

•15
Perils of the West and *The Germ*

Neal Hart's was the last outside production company to use the Shamrock Photoplay facilities. Shortly after the release of *Little Miss Bluebonnet,* June 13, McGeeney received "telegraphic dispatches" from his New York representatives, Bamburg and Levy, stating that they had sold rights to at least three of his scenarios submitted prior to the San Antonio flood. The "deal" for making the pictures—*Perils of the West, Jack of the Diamond A,* and *Down at Stien's Pass* (based on his first novel)—was "cleared on July 13," when he told the San Antonio press: "There must be something in '13' holding ill or good fortune....I believe strongly that the god of luck is smiling [on me] figuratively."

McGeeney wired William Karl Hackett in Los Angeles. Since his role as Henry Starr in *A Debtor to the Law,* Hackett had been the matinee idol in a couple of "society dramas"—*A Bird of Paradise* and *Mary's Ankle* (Paramount, 1920). "He was a rider and shooter of no mean ability and could thrill with the same ease that he charmed the fair ladies," said McGeeney. "He happened to be between contracts at the time and was willing to accommodate an old friend." For a heroine, McGeeney contracted actress and rodeo performer Eunice Goodrich; actor Harry Steiner would portray a desperado named "Tracey." McGeeney announced production of "a series of two-reel Hackett-Goodrich Westerns."

Perils of the West, first in the series, was "wide in its theme," its high points being "the greatest cattle scene ever filmed," "rustlers at work on a western range," "cowboy initiation of a tenderfoot," and a "real rodeo with its thrills of wild and trick riding of bronchos, steers and buffalo, in which a girl proves herself a champion broncho buster."

Perils also was the best plotted film of the series: Jim Raymond (Hackett), the young foreman on Patrick Livingston's ranch, is instructed to meet Livingston's wife and child, who are arriving on the stage. In town, Jim learns that a band of Apaches are raiding in that direction. The stage is attacked, which compels a transfer from coach to saddle. A running fight ensues. Daredevil riding brings Jim and his party to the ranch, followed closely by the Indians. In the course of the battle, the child runs from the house and hides in a well. Both father and mother are shot down in their attempt to bring her back. Jim rescues the child. Help finally arrives and the Indians are routed. As Livingston lies dying, Jim promises to look after the little girl.

A step-brother of Livingston's takes charge of the ranch and is appointed guardian of the child, which Jim objects to strenuously in view of his former employer's request. Jim finds evidence that the step-brother had incited the Indian attack in the hope of securing the ranch for himself. The step-brother flees with the child. Jim meets him face-to-face on the plains and kills him in a pistol duel. He finds no trace of the orphaned girl.

Jim looks after the ranch and continues his quest. Years later, while attending the annual rodeo, he meets Edna Sherwood (Eunice Goodrich). Miss Sherwood desires to enter the bronc-busting contest, but lacks the required fee, which Jim loans her. She wins the championship.

She has little recollection of her past, except that when a mere child she had been found in a cave in the hills by an old prospector and adopted by a rancher named George Sherwood. Sherwood had been killed by a notorious rustler, Tracey, and she had operated the ranch single-handed until a later raid by Tracey left her penniless.

Love blooms between Jim Raymond and Miss Sherwood. Both feel they have known each other in the past. Jim finds employment for her as a schoolteacher in the local settlement, and soon learns that Tracey is still in evidence when his own cattle begin to disappear. A posse is formed and a trap set for Tracey and

Jim Raymond (Hackett), foreman on Patrick Livingston's ranch, discusses the safety of the child with Livingston during an Indian attack. Scene from *Perils of the West* (1922).

William Karl Hackett, actress Eunice Goodrich, and McGeeney review script for *Perils of the West,* the first of a series of Hackett-Goodrich westerns produced by McGeeney in 1922.

his gang. The gang is caught red-handed; Tracey escapes. Jim pursues him across the border. The climax comes in desperate hand-to-hand combat atop a cliff. With a well-directed punch, Jim sends Tracey to his death in the chasm below.

The old prospector appears, confessing anxiety to meet Miss Sherwood after a long absence from the West. He identifies the dead Tracey as a confederate of the step-brother, who had hidden the girl in the cave where he had found her twenty years ago.

In a final touching scene, Jim takes Miss Sherwood to the old ranch house and well, where he reenacts the tragedy. It brings back memories and Jim is convinced that she is the little girl whom he had promised to protect. They marry and claim the Livingston property.

The Indian raid, rustling, cattle, and rodeo scenes were filmed on the 101 Ranch in Oklahoma, and McGeeney came away with an endorsement from the Miller Brothers, offering him a bonus of $20,000 to open a studio there. *Perils of the West* was distributed by Primrose Pictures Corporation of New York (the first Shamrock Photoplay to be accompanied by one-sheet, three-sheet, and six-sheet displays and advertising accessories such as slides, eleven-inch by fourteen-inch lobby photos, one- and two-column mats and cuts, thumbnail mats and cuts, and press book), and became a "double-feature treat" in theaters during the summer of 1922 alongside Charles Hutchinson's *Speed* and *Fighting Mad,* Herbert Rawlinson's *Nobody's Bride,* and Dustin Farnum's Arrow release, *The Trail of the Axe.*

McGeeney seriously considered the Miller Brothers' offer, but his forthcoming pictures called for Mexican border scenery. Snow in Oklahoma was a factor. A large number of Western filmmakers in California, Chicago, New York City, Fort Lee, New Jersey, and elsewhere had no studios of their own and used rental lots outside their immediate geographic regions with frontier streets, barns, blacksmith shops, and places where players could "overnight" while a production was in progress. McGeeney wanted to expand his Terrell Wells studio into such a facility, but urban sprawl, which "drove property values upward enormously," precluded it.

An aviation post had been established at San Antonio to assist United States forces on the Rio Grande in 1916. Kelly Field had been established as a training camp for World War pilots in 1917 and was becoming one of the largest such posts in the world. The city's population had "nearly doubled," and "fed on" army and aviation activity. Areas heretofore available for the Shamrock company's operations were being "built up rapidly."

McGeeney filmed the outdoor scenes for *Jack of the Diamond A* and *Down at Stien's Pass* on the Rio Grande, between Eagle Pass and Del Rio.

At Eagle Pass, he "tried to enlist some of the business men in establishing a moving picture studio," believing that he could "work out a profitable enterprise," as well as "get good advertisement for the community." He pointed out that a portion of *Heart of the Sunset* had been filmed there a few years previously, and with the "huge sheep and cattle ranches, wide open spaces and wonderful mountain scenery nearby in Coahuila, Mexico. . . no better setting could be found for the production of Wild West pictures."

The idea appealed to town promoters. However, they could not envision the small trading point and army village, with mostly Mexican inhabitants, becoming a mecca for the movie industry.

McGeeney tried again at Del Rio. He showed the 101 Ranch letter offering a $20,000 bonus to move his company to Oklahoma, but said there were "handicaps." He "dilated" on the fine scenic and climatic conditions, and "delineated" his plan to produce a dozen more Hackett-Goodrich Westerns. Said the Del Rio newspaper, "He arrived here Tuesday and a special meeting of the Chamber of Commerce was called at 10 o'clock Wednesday morning. . . Lew Rust in the chair. Secretary Robinson at once introduced Mr. McGeeney, who made a good impression by his personality and candid talk. . . .

"His proposition, in a nut shell, is this: The business men of Del Rio to form an association. . . to cooperate with him permanently. . . to furnish a lot, with a storage house and stage, and to pledge $15,000 on a profit basis of fifty-fifty. He puts up his experience, work, apparatus, etc. employing seven or eight workmen outside the actors. The sales [of twelve pictures] will amount to $4,000 each or thereabouts. . . . He calculates a return of $48,000. Deduct the cost of building storage house, etc. and the $15,000 from the association's half, and the estimated profits on these twelve pictures would be about $5,000. After these pictures are completed the corporation is at no further expense and gets the full fifty per cent. He stated that the Shamrock company could produce one two-reel picture a week. . . .

"Mr. McGeeney emphasized that, independently of the large profits accruing, Del Rio will be advertised through the movie journals and daily press.

"On motion, the chair appointed Walter Earnest, E.F. Measels and J. Berlin to confer with him and Secretary Robinson to examine into the proposition thoroughly before taking action."

The committee's report proved "favorable," but it needed "assurance" that the movie industry was "turning to Texas" and, by getting in on the ground floor, "Del Rio would reap the benefit." McGeeney thought the outlook was "obvious." Undeterred, he moved downriver to Laredo.

Laredo was a "very desirable site," laid out on the high banks of the Rio Grande in the vicinity of the San Augustín Plaza, old Fort McIntosh, and the Dolores Mission. It was originally Villa de San Augustín de Lareda, Mexico, founded by Colonel Tomás Sánchez de la Barrera y Gallardo of the royal army of Spain, who invaded the section at the head of a small expedition in 1750, exploring toward the mouth of the Nueces River. By 1836, when Santa Anna was entertained by a ball as he passed through on his way to the Alamo, it was a prosperous village of 1,700 Spaniards, mestizos and mulattoes. Following its incorporation under the laws of Texas in 1852, four years after the creation of Webb County, Americans slowly moved in, making many improvements.

Laredo now was a city with paved streets; an electric street railway; natural gas, electric lighting, and water systems; and a population of 25,000. Four railroads converged on the city, giving it excellent transportation facilities. A new concrete bridge, replacing the international tramway partially destroyed by a tornado in 1905 and burned in 1920, had been completed across the river to Nuevo Laredo at the cost of four million dollars. Fort McIntosh quartered 1,600 soldiers. Coal mines to the northwest produced thousands of tons annually. There were nearly three hundred producing oil wells in the same section. Both irrigated and dryland farming produced fruits, vegetables, feed, and cotton, and cattle raising was one of the main industries of its contiguous territory.

McGeeney spent a couple of days in Laredo renewing acquain-

Scene from *The Germ,* the "first Big Picture [seven-reeler] made in Texas," written and directed by McGeeney in 1923. Charles Swinton (McGeeney), a wealthy young scientist, comforts Nell, the "abused, unfortunate child of poverty and distress."

tances made during the filming of *A Debtor to the Law.* He "propounded to different business men's clubs" the opportunity to develop a great motion picture center there "by reason of the international atmosphere, natural scenery, light conditions and other advantages over the congested districts where other film makers are located." Said the Laredo *Times,* "He thinks the enterprise could be started with approximately $25,000. He believes a picture can be filmed here for half what it costs in other sections, and has a ready sale at a good profit for all the pictures he can make.... It is a matter local people might be giving some thought to."

A few days later, the *Times* announced, "P.S. McGeeney, director of the Shamrock Photoplays of San Antonio, has closed a deal with the Kiwanis Club to move his producing company here. The company plans to make eight 5-reel Westerns. Wm. K. Hackett and Eunice Goodrich are the leading players. The first will be *The Sheriff of Sunshine Valley.*"

Sunshine Valley was billed as "A Super Special Feature—Five Reels of Honest to Goodness Western ACTION, THRILLS, ROMANCE," by the Allied Distributing Corporation of New York. But it was the last of the Hackett-Goodrich series. The Kiwanis Club failed to raise the capital necessary to build a studio in Laredo, and McGeeney went back to San Antonio. Hackett returned to California and continued his career in films. He performed primarily in serials and westerns as a gang leader or henchman, until his death on October 24, 1948.

In June 1923, McGeeney wrote and directed the "first Big Picture made in Texas," entitled *The Germ*—a seven-reeler casting Max Wesell, Lillian Lawson, Myrl Hall, Wanda Wiley, Captain T.G. Hall, George Corey, and Ada Lewis, "all experienced in screen drama," and including "seventy extras, as well as approximately 200 school children who appear in one scene." He wanted Richard Barthelmess (of recent *Broken Blossoms,* with Lillian Gish; *Tol'able David,* and *Bond Boy* fame) for the leading role. But failing in this, he played the part himself (according to the publicity) "in a masterful manner."

The Germ was based on a scientific treatise by C.S. Warnock. The foreword gives the import of the picture:

"The governments and scientists of the world have given much thought to eugenics. Great races of men have been reared.

Wonderful improvements have been made in the animal and vegetable kingdoms. . . in antidotes and serums for preventing and curing disease. The churches have made strenuous efforts for the betterment of the world. But with all these beneficent influences at work, 'man's inhumanity to man' is as apparent today as it was 2,000 years ago. No real progress can be made while men's minds are permeated with jealousy, greed, anger, hatred and the many evil characteristics to which mankind is heir. These curses are symptoms of germs in the blood that can and must be eradicated before the world will be a fit place in which civilized human beings may dwell."

The story revolves around Charles Swinton (McGeeney), a wealthy young scientist who resides in a "garden of rare loveliness" (Japanese Sunken Gardens) and, concerned with man's fate, works untiringly to perfect a solution to the unhappiness in the world caused by certain germs that warp the human heart and soul. Lovely garden spots that bring appreciation of the beautiful in life are filmed, centering finally upon a rose being sapped by a worm, which is compared with a germ that mars the happiness and success of a young girl and saps life from her. A drunken father (Max Wesell) and his miserable, dismal home and desperate family—a wife and daughter, Nell (Myrl Hall)—are portrayed, Miss Hall "giving an admirable performance of the abused, unfortunate child of poverty and distress." A butterfly of a girl (Wanda Wiley), who has designs on the scientist but flits from one flower of romance to another, enlivens the theory that "the worm is a germ."

Critics who viewed a private showing of *The Germ* at the Palace Theater, July 9, called it "a picture lavish in San Antonio's beauties" and "a San Antonio film to uplift humanity." Overflowing crowds viewed it at the Opera House on July 26 with "a great deal of pride in the city and satisfaction in the spirit of the picture," and remembered the lines of the last fade out, "With peace in every heart the plowshare is mightier than the sword."

McGeeney and Warnock spent the week of August 6 in New York, where they visited the offices of the *Herald,* Primrose Pictures Corporation, and the Producers Security Corporation to obtain publicity and distribution of *The Germ* as a "Research Picture." The *Herald* praised McGeeney for "working hard to get recognition for Texas as a motion picture field" and producing "more than one hundred [?] movies." *The Germ,* however, received few bookings.

McGeeney came back to San Antonio, tired and disappointed. For some time, Mary McGeeney had doubted his future in the picture business. Too, she fretted about his long and repeated absences. McGeeney closed his Shamrock operations, and returned to Kansas.

The San Antonio *Light* printed this regret: "Many celebrities have lived in San Antonio—many have loved her quaint charm—but perhaps none have ever more ably expressed their affection than P.S. McGeeney. . . .

"Through him the whimsies of her river, the mystery of her ivy-covered adobes, and the romance of brushy hills which surround the city have been flashed around the world and back again. . . . In the last ten years he has been the means of bringing to San Antonio large Eastern companies and has handled almost a half million dollars of Eastern capital spent in the production of pictures. . . .

"He gives assurance that he will have several projects to occupy him next winter."

•16
Heart of Tucson

The McGeeneys spent the winter of 1923–24 among friends and relatives at Newton and St. Marys. The Newton *Journal* was "always glad to extend the praises of Kansas men and women who have gone out into the world and made a name for themselves," particularly to "P.S. McGeeney, who has become famous as an actor, author and motion picture producer. . . . Some of his pictures have taken high rank and many stars of filmdom were given their impetus under his direction." Mary enjoyed the idyllic existence.

McGeeney spent a great deal of time "collecting data" from the Mennonite families in Harvey and adjoining counties, and on the Cherokee Outlet in Oklahoma. By spring, he had two novels "nearing completion," the first based on the "bringing of hard wheat to Kansas by the Mennonites," the second on the 1893 "land rush" into the Outlet and his experiences as a railroader, express guard, and deputy U.S. marshal in Oklahoma Territory.

Meanwhile, he conferred with Henry J. Allen of the Wichita *Beacon*. Rumors flew that he had "interested influential men in Wichita and certain Newton men" in organizing a motion picture company in Kansas. The Newton *Journal* confirmed the rumors a few days later. "Mr. McGeeney has ideas well worked out for depicting outstanding features of Kansas and Oklahoma life on the silver screen. . . . One film will center on Kansas wheat, the other on the historic opening of the Outlet that he says will rival *The Covered Wagon* [the 1923 production of Emerson

Hough's popular novel, directed by James Cruze and acclaimed the screen's first epic western].

"Mr. McGeeney has been on the lookout for new screen faces. . . has on file applications from numerous people of more or less experience. . . with at least the ambition to try for parts in his screen dramatizations. He says he has in view some outstanding stars of the movie profession as leads, but it is possible that he will develop some Kansas and Oklahoma potential actors and actresses into stars."

It was San Antonio all over again. Mary McGeeney, her peaceful interlude irreparably disrupted, "went to live with her sister Kathleen in St. Louis." As one family member states, "Poor Pat was left to shift for himself."

Things might have been different had Mary McGeeney not departed too hastily. As in Del Rio and Laredo, the expected financial backing in Newton and Wichita was not forthcoming, and McGeeney drifted west to Santa Fe, New Mexico.

The Santa Fe *New Mexican* gives this resume of his sojourn there: "Tonight a meeting of the directors of the Chamber of Commerce and such other citizens as may be interested will be held to discuss with an experienced motion picture producer the feasibility of permanently establishing a motion picture studio here. This producer has been located in San Antonio, Texas, and has a number of successful films to his credit. His connections in the motion picture world are first class, and he carries with him evidence of his proficiency from the technical as well as other standpoints. . . .

"It is his impression that Santa Fe would be an ideal place for the production of western drama. While artificial lighting has progressed to the point where sunshine is unnecessary, it is very costly, and there are certain effects which can be produced only in out-of-door pictures taken in the sun. For scenery, this mountain and desert region is unsurpassed, while the ancient buildings, Indian pueblos, mission ruins and historic landmarks would furnish settings for any number of plots. The scenery of Southern California has been 'shot to pieces'. . . while Santa Fe surroundings are an inexhaustible variety.

"It is contended that motion pictures that would cost $50,000 or more to produce in California and New York studios could be staged just as effectively for a fraction of that sum in this vicinity. No great outlay would be required for studio facilities or elaborate settings, while local talent could be procured inexpensively.

"Incidentally, pictures taken here would be produced under a Santa Fe trademark and give this community additional publicity of a kind not to be had in any other way, and the success of one producer would inevitably result in others looking to this field. The money flowing in from the films would be spent locally and only those who know that millions of dollars are distributed in Hollywood annually and have made it a city of 150,000, when ten years ago there were less than 20,000, would appreciate what it would mean to Santa Fe to establish the industry successfully here."

Despite the *New Mexican's* appeal, McGeeney "batted zero." Chamber members desired "more business," of course, but Santa Fe's growth and prosperity were "substantial" without impairing its assets. Accustomed to low levels of service and low taxes in support of local government, the populace "scoffed" at any change that might cost them money or alter their Land of Poco Tiempo way of life.

McGeeney moved on to Tucson, Arizona. Some Zane Grey novels had been filmed in the vicinity. Famous Players-Lasky had just filmed portions of Harold Bell Wright's *A Son of His Father* there because of the "immense scenic advantages." These precedents favored McGeeney's proposal to produce a series of "special desert features" called Grand Canyon Pictures.

The *Arizona Daily Star* supported his idea. "There are some Tucsonans who laugh at you if you tell them that Tucson might some day have a six story business block. You can imagine what they say when they are told that a moving picture studio is a possibility.

"But things material move on in mighty peculiar and sudden ways, and it would not surprise many of us Tucson boosters if we woke up some morning and found Bill Hart, Tom Mix, Mary Pickford, Douglas Fairbanks and Charlie Chaplin 'shooting' the scenes of some Western drama, some tear-squeezing melodrama, or a rib-tickling, belly-shaking comedy.

"Why not? Haven't we better locations—ranches, ranges, mountain and canyon—than Southern California? Haven't we just as handsome residences as may be found in Los Angeles? And we have, right here in Tucson, just as good border-town stuff as you will find on the California border.

"All we need is the gumption to bring such an industry into town."

Which Tucson did. Said the Tucson *Daily Citizen:* "A committee of local business men have been appointed to consider the merits of Mr. McGeeney's plan. . . the status of his past work and his operations here. . . and have given a favorable report. A number of local business men have become financially interested. . . .

"The projected studio will occupy ten acres and the company will be capitalized at a quarter of a million dollars. . . .

"Associated with McGeeney are William Anthony Kennedy and B.A. Eyer, of Los Angeles. . . .

"McGeeney commented that his attention was first drawn to the unrivaled scenery of southern Arizona and excellent light for photography, in 1916 [while filming U.S. troops on the border], and that the result of certain tests made during a motor tour later [while filming *Among the Indians*] had decided him in selecting this city as an ideal site for a motion picture plant. . . .

"Explaining the cause for the motion picture industry locating in California, he said:

" 'Los Angeles was chosen, in the first place, on account of its climate, and principally because it was known in the East. But little thought was given to lighting and extensive and varied scenery. The early producers wanted a place where they could work the year round. The industry grew beyond expectations. Today the studios are crowded into Hollywood, the mountains and landscapes have been photographed again and again, and land values have reached a false high level. If anyone had thought of looking for the best place in the United States in which to make pictures, they would have chosen Tucson.' "

Later the *Citizen* reported, "What this Movie Master has done for San Antonio, he proposes to do here, and his first picture, he stated this morning. . . will be entitled *Heart of Tucson.* He is working on the scenario at present, and plans to put it into story form. He plans to comb the vicinity for talent to work on this feature, and to these embryo stars, he will add a nationally known actor, so that the picture will be assured a standing among the best in the country. [He mentioned] Blanche

McGarity, a San Antonio girl and one of his finds, who, at present, has heard the call of Los Angeles, and is continuing her work with companies on the coast. . . .

"*Heart of Tucson* will be made at the cost of slightly over ten thousand dollars, McGeeney says, while on the coast it would cost about twenty thousand. This smaller cost here is due to the fact that there is a longer working day with good light, that extras will cost less, that locations of a wide range can be reached in one to two hours, and that offers of cattle, mining camps and other locations, at no pay, have already been made.

"No date has been set for filming of the picture, but he expressed a hope to start within the next month."

Apparently McGeeney failed to obtain the services of Blanche McGarity, for he soon announced that "any Arizona girl with histrionic ambitions, providing that she 'screens well' and has the ability to act under training, will be given a chance to appear as the leading ingenue in *Heart of Tucson.*"

The *Citizen* explained, "This is not a contest, but an effort to secure the type of girl he requires. Any girl who wishes to apply has but to mail two photographs—a profile and full face view—with a description of herself. . . and whether she can ride, swim, dance, and her other accomplishments.

"Tucson Allen, the character to be portrayed, is a real daughter of the great southwest who is endowed with those feminine charms always admired by the sterner sex. . . . The choosing of an Arizona girl for this part is an honor conferred upon this state.

"The girl selected will be taught screen acting under Mr. McGeeney's supervision, without cost, and will receive a salary during the filming of the picture. Fame and fortune may be hers for the asking."

Applications poured in, with a girl yet to be selected in mid-June, when McGeeney finished his scenario.

The cast: Tucson Allen (recently returned from an eastern college); Diamond Allen (her aging father and owner of the Diamond Ranch); Phillip Everett (a ranch guest and Tucson's college chum, who is a good polo player but lacks ability with the books); Mrs. Everett (Phillip's mother); Skeets (the Diamond foreman); Lem Bow (the Diamond cook); Scottie (the ranch collie); Dick Branden (owner of the adjoining Coyote Ranch, who holds a mortgage on the Diamond, professes to be Allen's friend, and aspires for Tucson's hand); Smith (Braden's right hand man, but secretly head of a rustler gang); and a host of extras—cowboys, polo players (Everett's college friends), and spectators.

The story: Tucson Allen, whose word is as good as her bond, sees a herd of wild horses dashing by and exclaims, "I will marry the man that brings me the leader of that band." Branden tries; so do others. The man who does bring her the horse is Everett. He does not press his claim, however, since Tucson is needed by her father, who is failing in his ranch enterprise because of the rustling. Branden presses for either payment of the mortgage or Tucson's hand. The rustling increases. Diamond Allen, his back to the wall, is on the verge of giving his consent to the marriage, when Everett and his polo-playing friends (with the help of Skeets, Lem Bow, and Scottie the ranch collie) round up the rustlers and dispose of the mortgage holder for a thrilling climax.

The story was in novel form by the second week in July. The *Citizen* insisted, and McGeeney acquiesced. Commencing Sunday, July 13, *Heart of Tucson* appeared serially in the newspaper.

McGeeney recalled, "I sent write-ups on my forthcoming production and copies of the *Citizen* to the most important film trade journals in New York and to the big exchanges all over the country. This free publicity meant a great deal to Tucson, justly advertised her splendid scenic values and the unselfish cooperation of her citizens. Those are the big assets required in successful film making. . . and it was gratifying indeed to receive inquiries from some of the biggest releasers of motion pictures in the United States.

"Film Booking Offices of America wrote: 'We shall be very glad to negotiate for the release of your production, *Heart of Tucson,* after we have had an opportunity to review it'; and Arrow Film Corporation, by their vice president W. Ray Johnston: 'If you have a big picture in *Heart of Tucson,* we would of course be interested. . . . As soon as you are ready to send a print for screening we would be glad to consider release arrangements.'"

A number of inquiries were about the extent of his operations in Tucson. Toward the end of July, McGeeney told the *Citizen,* "I have contracted with three large distributing companies for 26 five-reel pictures. A series of 12 of these will be made first. Other contracts call for six and eight five-reel features, cash to be paid on delivery, and the companies have the right to place their okay on the male lead for each. I plan to secure an outstanding Western actor. . . and perhaps a 'heavy' and an expert cameraman.

"I am rushing final details for the production of *Heart of Tucson.*"

Then it happened. Dull, heavy pains in his chest and leg took him to St. Mary's Hospital. There, physicians diagnosed arteriosclerosis. McGeeney was put on a strict diet and firmly advised to follow a "slow life."

He disposed of his interest in Grand Canyon Pictures. *Heart of Tucson* was never completed—at least there is no record of it.

Stating only that he was in "bad health," McGeeney returned to Kansas.

•17
Politics, "Pancho," and "Allawishes"

From 1925 to 1927, McGeeney resided at 210 East Ninth Street in Newton. Mary came home. He recorded nothing of his exploits during these years, but it was in this period that he wrote many of his "Purple Sage" reminiscences and contributed articles to eastern magazines concerning his experiences in Mexico.

In 1925 the McGeeney twins left Tampico to work in the oil fields of Venezuela. Jack suffered a bout with malaria, and in 1927, he and Tom departed South America to join their brother Patrick, now living with his family at Long Beach, California. McGeeney's coronary condition seemed under control. Consequently, he journeyed with his wife to California to visit their sons and only grandchild, Mary Louise, whom he fondly called "wee Mary."

He surveyed Hollywood and Los Angeles, but "didn't like" what he saw. The era of pictures with sound-on-film recording and dialogue had dawned. In the silent movie, a minimum of dialogue was inserted between actual happenings. The picture itself had to tell the story and hold interest. It was a fast, compact form, always a "moving" picture. Movies with sound were quite different. Many producers opposed or were unable to afford the investment necessary for reorganization and equipment, and actors whose voices and ability to handle live dialogue were weak found themselves "looking at their hole cards."

McGeeney grew restless. He longed for Texas. Mary consented.

Back in Newton, they disposed of their Ninth Street property, and returned to their old home in San Antonio.

McGeeney's efforts to gain recognition for San Antonio as a motion picture center had not been in vain. In 1924 the Fox Film Corporation came from Hollywood to shoot exterior scenes in and around the city for *The Warrens of Virginia,* a seven-reel Civil War romance starring Wilfred Lytell and Rosemary Hill. San Antonio's sunshine and background attracted two other big productions: Metro-Goldwyn-Mayer's twelve-reel World War drama, *The Big Parade* (1925); and Paramount Famous Lasky Corporation's ten-reel Spanish-American War melodrama, *The Rough Riders* (1927), in which stars Noah Beery, George Bancroft, Charles Farrell, and Charles Emmett Mack, for various reasons, join the motley assortment of volunteers assembled on the Exposition Grounds. All see bloody action in Cuba and survive to attend the inauguration of Theodore Roosevelt as president of the United States.

McGeeney began work on a new novel, *Blood Moon*—a romance of the Southwest dedicated to the "sturdy, courageous Texas pioneers who tamed the Big Bend country. . . once the home of the Indian, later infested with cattle thieves and smugglers"; an empire of "high mountains, sandy deserts, unscalable barrancas and wild, wide open spaces that will someday become a Federal park and a grand rendezvous for tired business men, their families, hunters and nimrods fishing for the big blue cat in the Rio Grande as it echoes peacefully on its tortuous course though the deepest gorges of the Santa Elena, Mariscal and Boquilla canyons." As he predicted, the Seventy-fourth Congress took cognizance of the agitation by naturalists and passed an act on June 20, 1932, authorizing the establishment and maintenance of such a park. The Texas Legislature followed suit, appropriating 250,000 acres of state land and a million and a half dollars to acquire the remainder of the site under the supervision of the State Parks Board. In 1943 the state deeded some 788,862 acres in the southern extremity of the Big Bend of the Rio Grande in Brewster County to the federal government, and Texas had its first national park—the fifth largest in the United States and today termed by the National Park Service "one of the outstanding geological laboratories and classrooms of the world."

With *Blood Moon* in production, McGeeney concerned himself

with other sites and buildings related to the history and beauty of Texas. He lectured before the San Antonio Conservation Society and other historic-minded organizations, and wrote promotion pieces for the press. The Conservation Society had been founded in 1924 by a group of San Antonio women bent on preserving the old Market House. Failing in this, they turned their attention to the San Antonio River when, in 1926, they discovered that the large downtown riverbed was to be drained and covered with concrete. They saved the riverbed, the only meander to survive the rechanneling and tunneling in the city as the result of the 1921 flood. It eventually was landscaped; footbridges and river walks were constructed; many shops and restaurants were opened along the river; and this midtown section became known as "El Paseo del Rio."

Following the river victory, the society prevailed on the city to purchase the Spanish Governor's Palace. Society members supervised its restoration and filled curator positions. The Conservation Society would remain active in acquiring, restoring, and operating many other historic sites in the years to come.

McGeeney also dabbled in politics. He was a member of the Democratic party, the dominant party in Texas and as old as the state itself. Until 1928, Democrats had won every gubernatorial and presidential election, and the bulk of local elections except in isolated areas where traditionally pre-Civil War and Reconstruction Republicanism remained strong. On November 2, 1920, Harry McLeary Wurzbach had been elected to the Sixty-seventh United States Congress from the Fourteenth Texas District—the first native Texan to be a Republican representative. His antecedents had immigrated to Texas from Mannheim on the Rhine, Germany, when Texas was still a republic, living in Galveston, Fredericksburg, Austin, and San Antonio, where Wurzbach was born on May 19, 1874. He had been educated in San Antonio public schools and at Washington and Lee University, admitted to the bar in 1896, and served with the Texas Volunteer Infantry in the Spanish-American War. He resumed his law practices at Seguin, Guadalupe County, in 1900, where he was elected county attorney and, in 1904, county judge, and served four terms. McGeeney respected Wurzbach, and had openly supported his bid for the Sixty-eighth Congress in November of 1922. He wrote in the San Antonio *Light,* "Let us look over the congressional timber now on display, then select a man who is not a self-centered 'Grabalsky,' machine made, or who is afflicted with ringitus.

"During this dizzy, uncertain age of codes, rackets, and I might add crime, we need a real he-man and not a wrist watch as our congressman. A man who deems it a signal honor to represent all of the people. A man who is not picked in self-aggradizement and laden with promises of hypocrisy.

"From close observation some of our 'supine congressmen' no doubt were rank failures in business, and were elected not on merit, but through machines, cliques and lodges.

"Let us quit fighting over the postoffice site, or who will be the next dog catcher.

"Are you with me, Bosco? Now all together. Elect a two-fisted, square-shooter to be our congressman and show all the other states that Texas still believes in justice for all."

Many Democrats agreed, as evidenced in this letter from the Wurzbach Campaign Committee, dated November 10.

> My dear Mr. McGeeney:
>
> On behalf of Congressman Wurzbach and our organization, I take great pleasure in stating to you that he has carried the district by approximately 5000. According to our count, Bexar County gave him a majority of 3084. His re-election is due to a very great extent to the wonderful assistance given him by yourself and others, and I take this method, in his name and for myself, to sincerely thank you for all of us.
>
> At any time that Congressman Wurzbach or his friends can assist you in any way, you have only to make your request known and it will be cheerfully granted.
>
> With my kindest personal regards, and thanking you again, I beg to remain,
>
> Very sincerely yours,
> H.M. Hanson.

Wurzbach had been reelected to the Sixty-ninth and Seventieth Congresses. He was running for a fifth term in 1928, and McGeeney again bolted his party in Wurzbach's behalf. In addition he supported Herbert C. Hoover for president and Charles Curtis for vice president of the United States.

Not that McGeeney was "keen" for Hoover—though Hoover had been a tireless worker in behalf of millions of World War victims as food administrator under President Wilson and had served efficiently as secretary of commerce under both Warren G. Harding and Calvin Coolidge for the past seven years. It was because Hoover's running mate, Curtis, was McGeeney's "personal friend." Kansas born and a lawyer with American Indian ancestry, Curtis had served Kansas in the U.S. House of Representatives from 1892 to 1907, and continuously in the U.S. Senate since 1915.

On November 6, 1928, Hoover not only carried Texas, but won a smashing national victory over Democrat Alfred E. Smith (58.22 percent of the vote, with an electoral vote of 447 to 87). Curtis was the new vice president.

In the Fourteenth Texas District, Democrat Augustus McCloskey, a San Antonio lawyer and Bexar County judge, appeared to have defeated Wurzbach for the congressional seat. According to McGeeney, McCloskey was "supported by the San Antonio city political machine. . . . He served in Congress while Wurzbach contested the election. Several months later Wurzbach was declared the winner and McCloskey ousted." Afterwards, a San Antonio Citizens League was formed by prominent citizens to determine policy in campaigns and to nominate candidates. Conservative politically, the league declared itself against "machine rule," demanded only two terms for officeholders, and was a force to be reckoned with well into the 1930s.

Herbert Hoover took the oath of office as president on March 4, 1929. While celebrating the occasion in San Antonio, McGeeney learned that the once elegant Pierce-Arrow automobile which "so proudly bore Woodrow Wilson down Pennsylvania Avenue to the Capitol in Washington for his first inauguration in 1912" was for sale at a local used car lot. He contacted the dealer at once. "I was told that custom in Washington demands the president's car shall never be allowed to look old. When scratches appear on any part of the body or the enamel finish begins to lose its luster, or after being run about 5,000 miles, the car is recalled to the factory and sold to the highest bidder. So it was with this Pierce-Arrow of 1912.

"Charles Shelly, an admirer of Wilson, purchased the car and remodeled it into a hearse. After a long period of following the medical profession, covering up the doctors['] mistakes, the car, on account of its very long wheelbase and high speed, was con-

McGeeney (left) with his Pullman on wheels in front of the Municipal Building, San Antonio, on the eve of his departure for Washington, D.C. Mayor C.M. Chambers (center) and City Commissioners Frank Bushick and Phil Wright (right) and bidding McGeeney "bon voyage."

sidered a bit too unwieldly for transporting the dead. It was stripped to the chassis, placed on the used car market, and finally found its way to Texas.

"I bought it.

"The idea of carrying greetings from the mayors and governors along the route between San Antonio and Washington, in Wilson's old car, had occurred to me as one means of impressing on the people up East and North just what the great Southwest was like and had to offer. Too, being a personal friend of Vice President Curtis, I planned to talk over old times and hoped to redeem the Lone Star state in the eyes of the administration, since several political muddles had arisen that had put us more or less in a bad light with high officials. . . . I wanted to do my bit toward making the Republicans feel that Texas was with them and that they must be with Texas."

During the summer, McGeeney converted the former "first car" of the land into a "house on wheels": "I equipped it with Western Giant tires, an Exide battery, and every comfort of home except running water. It even had electric lights, an ice box and a Coleman cook stove, as well as a copious kitchen cabinet and folding chairs and bed, for most of the time I simply meant to stop by the roadside at night for a couple of dozen winks.

"The special coach body was built by Steve's Sash and Door company of San Antonio and painted with Glidden 'Speed-namel.' I had a picture of the Alamo painted on one side of the body, on the other side a sketch of the San Antonio municipal auditorium, and on the back of the coach the trademark of Gebhardt's chili and Mexican food products, as they were to be well advertised on the trip. Since it was impossible for me to see back through the truck while driving, I fitted up an electric bell, so that when I applied the brake, not only the 'stop' light flashed on, but the bell also rang a loud warning to any car behind that the truck was slowing down.

"The Mitla Mexican cafe of San Antonio provided a gift of Mexican pottery to Mrs. Hoover. The Gorn Stationery company sent a gift of fancy stationery to the two first ladies of the nation. Ed Kifer of the Public Service Company and Mr. Lockhart of the Household Furniture company also aided in making the trip possible.

"My journey would be made via Austin, Waco, Dallas, Fort

Worth [Texas]; Oklahoma City, Enid [Oklahoma]; Wichita, Newton, Emporia, Topeka, Leavenworth, Kansas City [Kansas]; Jefferson City, Missouri; Oregon, Chicago, Springfield [Illinois]; Indianapolis, Indiana; Columbus, Ohio; and Harrisburg, Pa. to Washington. I contemplated that the trip, barring bad weather, would take about thirty days."

On August 31, Mayor C.M. Chambers provided a "To Whom It May Concern" letter, as follows. "This will introduce Mr. P.S. McGeeney, a resident of the City of San Antonio . . . my personal friend for many years.

"Mr. McGeeney is leaving for an overland trip through the northern part of the United States, and any courtesies extended him while away from San Antonio will be appreciated by every member of the City Administration."

On the eve of departure — Labor Day, September 2 — McGeeney with his "motoring house" was photographed by the San Antonio *Light* in front of the municipal auditorium, while Mayor Chambers, Frank H. Bushick (San Antonio's historian) and Phil Wright, city commissioners, bid him "bon voyage."

He was asked by a *Light* reporter if he would have "any traveling companions. Certainly! A poisonous, but congenial Gila monster from the desert of Arizona, named 'Pancho' [for Villa], and 'Allawishes' [Aloysius], a chummy armadillo, who waves his queer little 'armored' paws about his head when Mr. McGeeney says 'Salute!' The Gila hasn't much of an appetite, eating nothing but two eggs a week, one on Tuesday and one on Friday, but Allawishes is described as 'a perfect little hog, who eats everything from soup to nuts.' The Gila monster will probably find its way into some Northern zoo, Mr. McGeeney says, while Allawishes is destined to become the pet of his niece in an Eastern city."

Upon arriving in Dallas, September 5, McGeeney was photographed with L.D. Selzer, assistant manager of the local branch of the Western Auto Supply, the firm which had furnished his Western Giant tires. Prior to leaving the city that night, he called on Mayor J. Weddy Tate for a letter of greeting to President Hoover. "The mayor was in session with the city commission," said the *Times-Herald,* "but he immediately suspended activities long enough to dictate a note of invitation to the 'big man in the little White House.' In substance his message was that 'in case you can ever find time to leave your official duties for a tour of the country, rest assured that the 300,000 people of Dallas will give you a most rousing and befitting welcome.' "

McGeeney recalled, "Upon explaining my mission to one 'prominent' citizen, the fellow studied a moment and then said, 'Hoover? Oh, yes; he's the man who makes sweepers!' "

At Wichita, Kansas, on September 13, he was the "guest of F.E. Good, manager of the local Western Auto Supply," where his traveling companions "caused a great sensation."

"Thus it went, all the way to Washington, which I reached on the 8th of October."

Said the Washington *Daily News:* " 'Presidential Greetings Car' is the pompous slogan prominently displayed on a lumbering Pierce-Arrow truck seen on 13th st. nw.

"Paintings of the famous Alamo of Texas history and of the new municipal auditorium at San Antonio adorn its sides, while gaudy letters on the elongated hood informs the passerby that it is none other than the motor and chassis of the car used by former President Woodrow Wilson in 1912. Oh, yes, it is an advertising stunt as you probably have guessed already. . . . P.S. McGeeney brought it here. It will be parked in front of the Western Auto Supply Company for several days while Mr. McGeeney displays his pet Gila monster and armadillo and chats with his long-time friend, Vice President Curtis."

McGeeney made his return westward via a southern route, visiting the "large Western Auto Supply Company headquarters at Memphis and at Little Rock," and reached San Antonio at the end of October, "mission accomplished." But he "never had a reason to ask any favors from the Republican party."

That same month the stock market crashed and prosperity turned into the worst depression America had ever known. Hoover was reluctant to take unorthodox measures to relieve the sick economy, and the money from federal loans to hard-pressed enterprises never trickled down to the needy. By the presidential election of 1932, Hoover's name was anathema to millions of Americans, many of whom were subsisting in tarpaper shack communities called "Hoovervilles."

McGeeney campaigned for New York's reform-minded governor, Franklin Delano Roosevelt, and Texas Congressman John Nance "Cactus Jack" Garner, his running mate. He struck up a correspondence with Roosevelt just prior to the November election by lauding his energetic cross-country campaign against the embattled Hoover. Roosevelt replied in kind from the Executive Mansion in Albany, November 3:

> My dear Mr. McGeeney:
>
> . . . I am taking a few moments to write and thank you for the splendid work you have been doing.
>
> From all reports I feel that we are going to have an overwhelming victory, but regardless of the result, I want you to know that I appreciate your loyalty.
>
> With best wishes, I am
>
> Yours very sincerely,
> Franklin D. Roosevelt.

All across the country, depression-stunned Americans responded eagerly to Roosevelt's promise of a "new deal." On November 8, they swept him into office by a margin of over 7,000,000 votes. Congress also went heavily Democratic.

McGeeney sent his congratulations to Vice President-elect Garner, and Garner replied from the Speaker's Rooms of the U.S. House of Representatives in Washington, November 14:

> Dear Mr. McGeeney:
>
> Thanks for your letter of the 9th expressing your good wishes and kind sentiments. It was very gracious of you to write me as you did, and I wish you to know I appreciate it.
>
> It was, indeed, a glorious victory for Democracy and is significant of the country's confidence. It will be an inspiration to all Democrats to give to our country the best of which they are capable.
>
> Sincerely and cordially yours,
> Jno. N. Garner.

At the end of November, McGeeney again wrote Roosevelt, congratulating him on his election to the presidency. He expressed his deep interest in the fate of the American Indian, and felt that the thorough study he had made of reservation conditions in 1919 qualified him for a position in the Office of Indian Affairs. In lieu thereof, due to his experience as a former deputy U.S. marshal and eight years supervising thousands of construction workers on the railway lines in Mexico, he aspired for appointment as warden of one of the federal penal institutions.

He also enclosed the following endorsements:

CHAMBER OF COMMERCE
San Antonio, Texas
November 16, 1932

Hon. Franklin D. Roosevelt
Governor of the State of New York
Albany

Dear Governor Roosevelt:

Mr. P.S. McGeeney, a loyal citizen of this city, contemplates making application for employment with the United States Government.

I wish to take this opportunity of stating to you that I have known Mr. McGeeney for a number of years and know of no one for whom I have a higher regard. Mr. McGeeney is extremely capable, of sterling character, and I firmly believe that with his qualifications would be suitable for any type of employment put under his jurisdiction.

I therefore bespeak for him your very serious consideration.

Yours very truly,
H.H. Ochs
PRESIDENT

From the city administration of San Antonio:

Dear Mr. Roosevelt:

It is with gratifying pleasure that we commend to you for your earnest consideration one of our esteemed citizens Mr. P.S. McGeeney for an appointment as Warden at one of our penal institutions.

His long successful business career, the handling of large numbers of men on construction, and last but not least his able assistance to one of our Ambassadors, the late Henry Lane Wilson, in the handling of delicate situations in Mexico should not be passed over lightly, and should be rewarded. . . .

Our sincere greetings, and wishing you health and happiness in your great endeavor to return prosperity to our land. We beg to remain,

Sincerely yours,
C.K. Quin*
Mayor of San Antonio

Frank H. Bushick
Commissioner of Taxation

Jake Rubilo
Commissioner of Parks and Sanitation

* Quin had become mayor following the death of C.M. Chambers.

Phil Wright
Commissioner of Fire and Police

Paul Steffler
Commissioner of Streets and Improvements.

Sheriff Albert Hausser of Bexar County wrote Vice President-elect Garner at his home in Uvalde, Texas, on November 19:

My dear Mr. Garner:

It is with great pleasure that I am introducing to you Mr. P.S. McGeeney for your kind consideration.

Mr. McGeeney is a staunch, loyal and lifelong Democrat, a man of keen judgment, business experience, extensive travels, and an honest, capable and moral citizen.

His experience as a Deputy U.S. Marshal in the old Indian Territory and his many direct contacts with the different Indian tribes since would, I am sure, be of great value to our government, and I recommend him for an appointment in the Indian service.

His eight years residence in Mexico, where he was of valuable assistance to Ambassador Henry Lane Wilson in effecting the release of many unfortunate American citizens who were imprisoned there, were most commendable.

In 1912, Mr. McGeeney, unaided, effected a settlement between the Mexican government, the National Railways and the striking Foreign Railroad employees. In all cases, he gave his time and talents gratis. His splendid free lance support during the past election should not go unrewarded. I shall appreciate any favor you may show him.

Wishing you and your good family health and happiness, I beg to remain

Sincerely your friend,
A. Hausser
Sheriff.

McGeeney heard nothing from Garner. Roosevelt wrote from the Executive Mansion in Albany, December 3:

My dear Mr. McGeeney:

Your message of good will and congratulations pleased me very much. It is my earnest wish that I may always deserve the confidence which has been shown in me.

Yours very sincerely,
Franklin D. Roosevelt.

There being no mention of his endorsements or an appointment, McGeeney made inquiry, which brought this reply from Hyde Park, February 8, 1933:

> My dear Mr. McGeeney:
>
> Mr. Roosevelt has received your letter of January 17th, and the recommendations regarding a possible appointment in the new administration.
>
> It is, of course, too early to take this up, but I can assure you that Mr. Roosevelt has directed that your application be placed in a special file to be brought to his attention when he considers such matters.
>
> Very sincerely yours,
> Louis Howe
> Secretary to Mr. Roosevelt.

McGeeney remained hopeful. However, other inquiries to Roosevelt brought "only promises of consideration from Mr. Howe. . . . My esteem for our President-elect deteriorated."

So did the country's condition. By inauguration day, March 4, 1933, nearly one third of the nation's labor force was out of work, and those who had jobs were working for as little as ten cents an hour. The run on banks had become acute. Malnutrition was a fact of life.

McGeeney's discontent grew with "what happened the following months in our nation's Capitol."

•18

El Diablo Cojo (The Limping Devil)

During his famous "First Hundred Days" in office, President Roosevelt easily persuaded Congress to create such agencies as the Civilian Conservation Corps (CCC), Federal Emergency Relief Administration (FERA), Agricultural Adjustment Administration (AAA), Tennessee Valley Authority (TVA), Farm Security Administration (FSA), and the National Recovery Administration (NRA) to alleviate the nation's social and economic miseries. Later, more agencies were formed, including the Securities Exchange Commission and Social Security Administration. "The only sure bulwark of continuing liberty," FDR argued, in his radio broadcast "Fireside Chats," "is a government strong enough to protect the interests of the people."

Labor dubbed the NRA the "National Run Around." McGeeney agreed: "The nation needed more than a series of 'alphabet agencies' to solve its woes. . . .

"On account of my health, and being a lover of the great outdoors, I took to the road. . .made my own surveys."

On August 31, he drafted a lengthy report to "old Pass the Buck" Roosevelt at the White House. He stated in part, "All men are born equal. Power, position or riches are not taken into consideration by the Great Master of the Universe.

"When I address a man, no matter who he may be, I expect an answer. I decline to take cognizance of the communications signed by Mr. Howe, and I am returning the same to you. . . .

"I could advance several reasons why you have not appointed

me to one of the offices which I have applied for, but will not. . . .

"Age is no barrier. In looking back over the pages of history, I find that anyone can be a president, vice-president, congressman or cabinet officer. . . whether ninety or one hundred years old. . . from any walk of life and without education or business qualification. . . knowing nothing of international law or diplomacy.

"Our days of pioneering are over. Our big corporation of approximately one hundred and twenty million people need business executives, real he-men, to handle the gigantic affairs of our commonwealth. . . who can and will uphold our constitutional rights. . . . Our appointees are always aware of the fact that four years or eight years, at the most, will end their stewardship. Are these men giving their entire time to the affairs of their office? Anyone can guess the answer. Their personal affairs come first.

"A great number of our appointees and a vast number of Government employees are dull, inexperienced, and sometimes impudent. They remind me of a story which is worth repeating.

"A gentleman wishing to settle a point or two on art approached the information desk of a certain public library. 'Where,' he asked, 'shall I find something on Correggio [the Italian painter] and his Flight into Egypt?' 'Everything about aviation is in room 121,' responded the clerk.

"This is how some of our appointees draw their breath and, I was going to write salaries, but pensions is a more appropriate word. . . .

"The man on the outside cannot understand what is taking place on the inside; nevertheless, if he is an unbiased thinker and keen observer through long experience in contact with all classes of people, he can arrive at a logical solution of the happenings taking place within. . . .

"The NRA to date is a rank imposition upon the rights of the people. Such business, from my viewpoint, has become a monopoly. What has happened to the Anti-trust laws? Will the Blue Eagle lay a golden egg, or will she hatch out a big Red Eagle?

"Unemployment? No doubt, you are gleaning from the files of the Union Labor Organizations, the number of unemployed published by the press. I estimate that we have approximately thirty million unemployed. Have you taken the census of the unemployed who are not affiliated with any labor organization? Several million unemployed are too proud to give their names into those so-called relief bureaus. They do not want *charity;* they want *work.*

"The destroying of foodstuffs, and the plowing up of growing crops is a damnable crime when starvation and privation are running rampant. . . .

"Farm relief seems to be the big issue of the day, and it reminds me of the old saying—"The cart before the horse." One farmer can raise enough foodstuff to supply several hundred families. If the several hundred families are unemployed the farmer is out of luck. Put the unknown, unskilled unemployed regardless of age, with or without dependents, to work at fair wages and the farmer will have all the relief he needs.

"Old man Depression has cornered the business of the nation.

"Old man Detour has a first and second mortgage on all our highways.

"Old man Manana [indefinite future] controls all the work.

"Get rid of them—then perhaps prosperity will sneak around the corner."

McGeeney dwelt extensively on other subjects: "Broken Promises" (of a president who claimed to be "always glad to have any citizen feel free to write me, and to give a frank and direct reply"); the "Tree Army" (CCC); "Elephantitus and Dam Mockery"; "Philippine Independence"; "No Recognition of Russia"; "Millionaires"; "Souls of Bondage"; "Open Season on Bankers"; and "Dictator Johnson" (U.S. Senator Hiram Warren Johnson of California, "a volcano of perpetual eruption, belching fire and smoke," and sponsor of the congressional act prohibiting private loans to nations in default of their debts to the United States).

McGeeney offered all of this as "constructive criticism." But it ended his communication with the White House.

Afterwards, he put the transmissions into manuscript form, entitled *Don't Read.* Submitted to E.P. Dutton and Company, of New York, it evoked the following response from Editor Merton S. Yewdale:

> Dear Mr. McGeeney:
>
> Thank you for sending the correspondence which has passed between you and President Roosevelt. You certainly have dealt

> realistically with the questions that are agitating the American mind. Not many men would go to the trouble of letting the Chief Executive of the Nation know that a certain citizen has very definite and constructive ideas. It was mighty good of you to send me your book.

However, Editor Yewdale declined acceptance, and *Don't Read* was privately printed in San Antonio. It was widely distributed.

Governor Harold G. Hoffman of New Jersey wrote from Trenton, "It is heartening to know that you disagree with the course [the nation is taking] and that you take the trouble to say so." Governor Eugene Talmadge of Georgia was "glad to know that you concur in my views and my fight to wake up the American people. . . . I am convinced that the time has come for action and that the real principles upon which our Government was founded are at stake."

McGeeney had thousands of sympathizers. But many labeled him a "crank." "I like the word for its literary meaning," he said. "A crank is a man who does his own thinking—a something that starts the machinery into operation." He maintained that free enterprise and careful management of state and local budgets, not federal spending, would do more to restore prosperity.

This also was the view of former businessman Alfred M. Landon, a 1912 Bull Mooser and Progressive Republican, who had been elected governor of Kansas in 1932 despite the sweeping Democratic victories. Governor Landon already was doing for Kansas—competently, constitutionally, and economically—much of what the New Deal meant to do nationally.

On Sunday, October 1, 1933, McGeeney appeared at Newton to address a mass meeting of Harvey County workers at Athletic Park "for the purpose of perfecting an organization whereby the unemployed might take some steps to solve their problems, with the cooperation of their employed brothers." Other speakers included Virgil A. Gendron, general secretary of the Railroad Telegraphers, and R.E. Fuller, a Landon proponent and representative.

The Harvey County *News* reported, "R.E. Fuller . . . called attention to Governor Landon's acts to benefit the laboring man.

"Calling specific attention to the attitude that 'if they can afford a car they do not need work,' Mr. Fuller said Mr. Landon evidently understood the working man's position better than anyone, as one of his first acts was to secure the reduction of the auto tag tax.

"Mr. Fuller also commended the Governor for his 'fearless chopping at the roots of graft, heedless of where the chips may fall,' and called upon all present to stand loyally behind the Governor and other officials in these trying times....

"Virgil A. Gendron...gave an interesting and hopeful talk about the causes of depression and what he believes will be one remedy....[Hard pressed by competiton from trucks, cars, buses, airplanes, and oil pipelines, the rail companies were carrying a lower and lower percentage of the nation's freight and intercity passengers. The current move by industry leaders to establish the Association of American Railroads by merging the two existing policy setting bodies—the Association of Railways Executives and the American Railway Association—would provide more effective leadership in streamlining day-to-day operations; i.e., eliminating widespread duplication of costly services and facilities of some 170 separate railroad companies in the United States].

"P.S. McGeeney...covered the time from the railroad trouble in Mexico down to the present and ended with a plea for unified and intelligent action on the part of workers to help themselves....He drew a hearty round of applause by thanking the crowd for patiently listening to him 'blow off.'

"The unemployed are to open and maintain their own exchange and cooperate with other relief measures...each to do his bit to help keep the people from desperate conditions which sometimes make temporary outlaws of the best of men."

Back in Texas, McGeeney blasted the "alphabet" government in Washington in William Randolph Hearst's San Antonio *Light*. Hearst, at the height of his wealth and influence, possessed two motion picture companies, eight radio stations, thirteen magazines, and twenty newspapers, including the Liberal-Democratic *Light* which he had bought in 1924. Using the sensational journalistic tactics that were his lifelong hallmark, Hearst molded the opinions of millions of Americans on politics and war, and had been instrumental in securing the nomination of Roosevelt for president in 1932. His increasingly conservative and isolationist beliefs now clashed with Roosevelt's policies, and the *Light* welcomed McGeeney's contributions.

One example is sufficient:

With gratifying interest I read Mr. Hearst's ably written article entitled "A Supine Congress." His comments and suggestions embodied there should be read and taken to heart by the right thinking people of our land. Reading between the lines, I infer that history has again repeated itself, and we have returned to "taxation without representation."

His article confirms my own deductions made of the congressional situation during my last trip to Washington, "we have approximately nine hundred senators and representatives; but are they representing the government 'of the people, for the people and by the people?' "

How can they, when the lobbyists representing big industries are dominating them?

The immortal Travis drew a line upon the floor of the Alamo with his saber—every man crossed that line, except one—even the disabled Bowie from his sick-cot begged to be carried across.

Today Mr. Hearst has taken the place of the great Travis and with a pen he has drawn a line. Will you cross that line to support his standard, or are you going to be numbered with the slackers and turn your country, your birthright, over to a few moguls steeped in greed, self-aggrandizement and despotic power?

P.S. McGeeney.

Nonetheless, President Roosevelt achieved popular endorsement of his policies. Millions of Americans, in a period of rising business activity, felt that their personal lot had been improved by the New Deal. Campaigning against Governor Landon in 1936, Roosevelt again toured the country, simply asking, "Are you not better off than four years ago?"

No one doubted that Roosevelt would be reelected; the question was the extent of his victory. The Republican party's cries of calamity and grim warning that "America is in peril" held no terror for the coalition of farmers, union men, blacks, and dispossessed on their way to the poorhouse. The popular vote on November 3 was 27,752,869 for Roosevelt and 16,674,665 for Landon; the electoral vote was 523 to 8. Roosevelt carried every state except Maine and Vermont, while Democrats captured seventy-seven percent of the House and seventy-nine percent of the Senate and won on the state and local levels in unprecedented numbers—on their own merits and on Roosevelt's coattails.

McGeeney suffered a further defeat—he was unable to place his novel, *Blood Moon,* with a publisher. Yet he endured. The history of the Lone Star State occupied his time and talents.

In 1936, in the midst of the Depression, Texas celebrated the centennial of its independence from Mexico, with fervor and extravagance. The state legislature and the United States Congress each appropriated $3,000,000 for the project. The centennial turned Texas into big business and convinced America it wasn't just "some place between Chicago and the Pacific where people rode horses."

The celebration began at Gonzales in November 1935. In December, San Antonio held a series of pageants to commemorate the siege of Bexar. El Paso featured an Indian Tribal Ceremonial in January 1936, and Galveston a Mardi Gras in February. Houston celebrated its founding, Texas Independence, and the Battle of San Jacinto in March and April. The two most widely visited observances were the Centennial Exposition at Dallas and the Frontier Centennial at Fort Worth. The Dallas exhibition occupied fifty buildings in the State Fair Park and featured the "Cavalcade of Texas," a historical spectacle presenting four centuries of Texas history. The Frontier Centennial at Fort Worth featured the "Winning of the West." Historic buildings and forts were restored and statues erected to a score of Texas heroes; every county received a marker bearing the date of its creation and the source of its name; guide maps to historic spots were furnished centennial tourists; the U.S. government issued commemorative three-cent stamps and half-dollars; and many newspapers offered special anniversary editions.

McGeeney traveled the state, writing features and articles. In the meantime, he completed a new novel, entitled *El Diablo Cojo* (The Limping Devil). Published in a Texas Centennial Edition, in May, by the Standard Printing Company of San Antonio, it was dedicated to the "Great Southwest, peopled with the best and the worst . . . but above all, adventuresome, honest, home-loving men and women, stripped of the hypocritical veneer of social environment, standing clean and true, with the hearts of children and souls that respond to the voice of religion like the arrow responds to the string of the bow—loving wisely—hating fiercely—their code their law." Thousands of copies were sold in Texas, New Mexico, Arizona, and Kansas.

El Diablo Cojo was also well-publicized. The San Antonio *Southern Messenger* called it "a mystery story, the action centering in southwest Texas in the hill country near Rocksprings and the Devil's Sink Hole, and abounds in names and anecdotes of well-known ranchers and cowboys. . . . It is written in scenario style, bringing out the dramatic values sharply, a characteristic not to be denied an author whose work was for many years that of a motion picture director."

Reviewer Paul Adams, of Radio Station KABC, considered it something "different from *Texas Grasses*. . . . *El Diablo Cojo* is flavored with generous supplies of romance and humor. There are no dull pages. From the first sentence to the last, the story moves with a rush. The author, P.S. McGeeney of San Antonio, who writes under the colorful pseudonym of Purple Sage, is no slavishly imitative writer, which a sample sentence or two will show:

"'One of the dudes was a prissy old maid, Miss Abigail Wantem. Her face was a cross between that of an owl and a pelican. Large horn-rim glasses hooked over her ears; her hair was a steel grey color, which she wore in ringlets like a sixteen year old girl. Her long, flat form reminded one of a stake and rider fence. She was of uncertain age and quite wealthy in her own right. She traveled at will, and the brown skin lady was her maid.'

"Mr. McGeeney has been an actor, a motion director and scenario writer. . . . And last, but not least, his early life as a deputy U.S. marshal in the Indian Nations, his many narrow escapes from outlaw guns, his eight years of thrilling adventure in Old Mexico, are subjects he has hidden in the archives of his memory. . . . If he were to write his autobiography, what a story that would make!"

Editor Edward M. Pooley, of the El Paso *Herald-Post*, read *El Diablo Cojo* with "a great deal of interest. . . . It seems to me there is a screen story in it."

The Newton *Journal* likewise thought that the book "should be screened and that Pat should realize from the royalties."

McGeeney received praise from readers everywhere, including Governor Landon, at Topeka; James B. Duffy, passenger traffic manager of the Atchison, Topeka and Santa Fe Railway Company's Coast Lines, in Los Angeles; and Maury Maverick, Texas' Twentieth District congressman, in Washington, D.C.

The finest comment came in a March 30, 1937, letter from

Frank H. Bushick, who, in 1934, had presented a panoramic pen picture of folk and places when San Antonio was the wide-open town of the 1870s–1890s, under the title *Glamourous Days:*

> My dear McGeeney:
>
> I am writing to tell you that I and my two boys have finished reading your splendid book, *El Diablo Cojo*. . . . I have quite a collection of Texas books and this is the only one so far that has been passed from granddad to son and from son to grandson for reading in succession. . . with any degree of enthusiasm. There is not a dull page in the book. You have truly caught the open heart spirit of the cow camp and life in general among the people of Southwest Texas. The delineation of character is so true to nature that we can see them as plainly as if we knew them. My ten year old grandson, Bobbie, talks of "Ebony Joe" and "Vinagaroon" as if they were pals of his. . . .
>
> It is the function of a writer to make reality more real and so emphasize the prosaic and ordinary things in life as to make them take on a new and added interest, finally adding to the reader's storehouse of information and appreciation of things as if he had overlooked something on all previous contacts. When a book can give a man a new sense of satisfaction in that manner the writer has achieved the highest art of writing. There isn't many of us who can gild the rainbow or add tint to the lily and unless a writer can do that he better not spoil his good white paper. I congratulate you upon your accomplishment in this respect. . . .
>
> Your insight into human nature and the many chapters vibrating with life and incident make your book a rich contribution to Texiana.

•19
California Sunset

Weary of Patrick Sylvester's political controversies and "vagabonding," Mary McGeeney went to California to be near her sons and their families. Tom had married Ester Lelea Brown, a Long Beach girl, in 1932. In March 1938, Ester bore him the first McGeeney grandson, Thomas Michael.

McGeeney wrote from San Antonio, March 26:

> Dear Tom:
>
> Congratulations to you, and my best wishes to your good wife.
>
> I hope wee Tom mick will be the hoth [sic] of a boy.
>
> He arrived on the first day of Spring and should be called "Spring" McG.
>
> Love to all,
> Dad.

He postponed going to California, because he was at work on a voluminous novel entitled *El Capitan* and involved in the development of the Frontier Times Museum, operated by J. Marvin Hunter at Bandera, forty miles northwest of San Antonio. Hunter also published *Frontier Times,* a monthly magazine "devoted to frontier history, border tragedy and pioneer achievements," and had invited McGeeney to submit some articles. McGeeney "generously supported the work Hunter was trying to do," and was a good friend of Hunter's boyhood companion—a Kerr County native and collector of old rare photographs—Noah H. Rose.

Frontier Times had been established at Bandera in 1923, and the museum in 1927, when Hunter used a small house in which to exhibit his collection of relics from Texas and the Southwest. In 1934 he constructed a larger building of native stone, fossils, petrified wood, and stalagmites and stalactites from Bandera County caves. A new addition called Chisholm Trail Hall had been completed in January 1938.

Hunter wrote McGeeney on January 26:

> Dear Colonel McGeeney:
>
> A thousand thanks to you. . . . I am certainly proud to place your name on the beautiful red granite column at the entrance of the new building. It is such loyal friends as yourself that is making it possible for me to carry on, and I want you to know that I appreciate your cooperation and assistance.
>
> I hope you can come to the "housewarming party" when the formal dedication takes place.

The "housewarming party" was held on Saturday, May 28. And what a day it was! McGeeney arrived early for the "patter"; hundreds toured the museum and swarmed over the grounds. The program began at "ten o'clock sharp" to the tune of "The Arkansas Traveler," followed by a Chisholm Trail square dance, the Arkansas clog, old fiddle tunes, a "Diamond Jim" rendition with banjo, and old songs by the popular Wiemers Family. Mrs. Julia Chisholm Davenport of New York, granddaughter of Jesse Chisholm, dedicated a stone tablet in his honor by breaking a bottle of water from the Chisholm Spring in Oklahoma. Dean T.U. Taylor, "the grand old man" of the University of Texas and Chisholm biographer, summarized Jesse's exploits.

The Bandera Parent-Teachers' Association served chicken and dumplings and barbecue lunches at thirty-five cents per plate. Governor James V. Allred delivered the 1:30 P.M. address, and during the remainder of the afternoon the crowds were treated to a "Cotton-Eyed Joe" dance, schottische, spinning wheel and shingle-making demonstrations, rope twirling, bow and arrow shooting, log chopping, and horseshoe pitching. The party ended with a barn dance at 8:00 P.M., in Mansfield Park, under the auspices of the Bandera fire department.

The years had crept up on McGeeney like ghosts in the night. He "took up vagabond quarters" on South Flores Street. The San

Antonio *Light* of September 6 noted: "Our old motion picture director friend . . . who has long deserted the field to Paramount and Fox . . . is still seen around occasionally"—touring in his Willys-Knight automobile.

McGeeney spent most of his time in the Bandera Hills. By winter, *El Capitan* was on its way to an "Eastern publisher"—all sixty-nine chapters of it—and he had begun work on three additional novels, *Chief Geronimo, The Bells of San Xavier,* and *My Tumbleweed.* His "old heart was acting up again." In January 1939, he entrained for California to be with his wife and grandchildren, and to deliver his memorabilia to his sons.

The Long Beach *Press-Telegram* made much of the occasion. Cameras clicked while the "gray-haired, genial author-vagabond with the wit of the Irish" thumbed through his "adventure-packed scrapbook" and related his "hair-raising experiences" as a deputy U.S. marshal in Oklahoma and superintendent of construction on the railways in Mexico. "The 1886 model 38–56 Winchester rifle was presented to him by the Wells Fargo Company when he frustrated the attempt of three desperados to rob a train at Ponca, Indian Territory; the Bisley 45-calibre Colt was given to McGeeney by one of the bandits, Henry Starr, in 1920; the spurs once belonged to Pancho Villa."

The newspaper summarized his debut in the motion picture making business in Mexico and his photoplay operations at San Antonio. "He has written more than a hundred short stories [articles], plays and scenarios. Among his books are *Down at Stien's Pass, Down at the Cross Timbers, The Power of Love* and *El Diablo Cojo*. . . . He has a number of novels, mostly western, as yet unpublished," and three in the making, which he "expects to put on the market in the near future."

After a brief rest on the Coast, McGeeney began "feeling better," but he longed to be away from the "clubs, cafes, social functions and raspy, discordant voices" of big city life. "I missed those dear, red-blooded men and women of the Great Southwest. . . . I would that it were possible [to] be among them for the end—loving as they love; fighting as they fight; hating as they hate; dying as they die, in the rosy glow of a New Mexico morn, in the dim twilight of a dying Arizona day, or in the cool of a Texas midnight morn."

It was not to be, however. Back in the Bandera Hills, he completed *Chief Geronimo, The Bells of San Xavier,* and *My Tumbleweed,* and was still shuttling *El Capitan* among publishers, when San Antonio friends advised his sons at Long Beach that he "wasn't caring for himself." The man, they reported, was "in poor health—virtually starving."

His sons insisted, and McGeeney returned to California. His trunk, filled with manuscripts and personal effects, and his Willys-Knight automobile were shipped to Long Beach on the Union Pacific railroad. In September 1943, he entered a rest home at Artesia, where he died October 15 from coronary occlusion, at age seventy. He was buried in the Calvary Cemetery and Mausoleum on Whittier Boulevard in Los Angeles.

Patrick Sylvester McGeeney's exploits and adventures might have passed into oblivion had he not recorded them as *Purple Sage*.

Index